THE END OF US

A TRUE STORY OF DEATH, DECEPTION AND CHINA'S DEADLY GRIP ON US HEALTHCARE

TONY PAQUIN

This book is dedicated to my wife, Keisha, the love of my life. She has supported me through every twist and turn of this adventure, at work and at home.

I would not have made it here without you.

CONTENTS

PREFACE

When COVID ravaged the country and the government kicked its vaccination program, Operation Warp Speed, into high gear, my small medical supplies company was called upon to provide the needles and syringes needed to deliver the vaccine to hundreds of millions of Americans. That mission became a saga of twists and turns, high stakes and low points, and many failures, setbacks, and struggles. And while we ultimately succeeded despite the odds, we saw firsthand two serious problems with America's medical supply chain: how fragile it is and how we depend far too much on China and other distant and sometimes hostile nations to keep the supply chain running.

America's decrepit manufacturing base makes us vulnerable. We just don't produce the stuff we all need to keep us healthy and alive.

For many people, this discussion may seem academic. For me, it is personal. It takes me back to the twentieth century, when I grew up amidst the vitality and independence of American industry. My father, Raymond, was a senior executive at General Motors, in Flint, Michigan. He was a plain-talking man, smart but not formally educated, moral, hardworking, and committed to his family. He had jet black hair combed straight back, a ruddy complexion, smoked a pack of Kent cigarettes a day and had a cocktail most nights when he got home. He never missed a day of work—until a near-fatal heart attack sidelined him.

My dad was stocky and tough. "Hard times make strong people and strong people make good times," as the saying goes, and Ray and his generation were tough people who lived through hard times (the Great Depression, World War II, etc.) and managed to make good times out of it, laying the groundwork for a booming economy and a thriving middle class—the American dream come to fruition.

He grew up during the Depression, served in World War II, and saw how the American industrial powerhouse revved up to respond to the global threat of Nazi Germany and Imperial Japan.

After the war he embarked on a career in the automotive industry, the era when Jimmy Hoffa was coming up in the Teamsters. The union guys and the company guys were sometimes at odds but had a lot in common—hardworking people who believed in self-reliance, who wanted to put food on the table and live in a peaceful, prosperous nation that lived up to its values.

This "greatest generation," through dogged determination and commitment to country, built the strongest economy the world has ever seen.

My dad wouldn't recognize the world we live in today. He would be aghast at how deindustrialization and globalization have sapped the nation of its self-reliance and vitality, not to mention millions of jobs. He would see, correctly, that America and Americans are vulnerable in a way they were not in his day.

I was born into this manufacturing epicenter—Flint, Michigan—in 1958. Life was good. The economy was booming. Employment was high. Ray, that streetwise, poor kid from Detroit with no college education, was a plant manager at a factory employing over fifteen thousand people. Like millions of Americans, his lot in life was improving.

But by the mid-seventies, things began to change. The big automakers were cutting costs and putting the squeeze on workers. Companies started locating more and more of the assembly process overseas.

By the time the eighties came, American industry was in a steep decline, and I had a front-row seat. In Michigan, Toyota and Honda muscled in on GM and Ford, which continued to set up factories abroad themselves. Charles Wilson, CEO of GM, said in 1953, "As goes General Motors, so goes the nation." His statement was prescient.

I was in my twenties, and the recessions of the 1980s hit Flint, already reeling from urban decay and the adverse effects of globalization, hard. Inflation reached a startling 13 percent and unemployment was in the double digits. Massive layoffs further devastated my once-thriving community.

I was the first of my brothers to never work in a factory, and I quickly found, like thousands of others, that I had to leave Michigan. In 1982, when I was twenty-four, I left Michigan for greener pastures. I founded and held leadership roles in multiple companies in the software and healthcare fields. I cofounded and was the CEO of Agency One, which after being acquired by CNA Financial Corporation became Vertafore, one of the largest software companies in the insurance industry. I later formed and served as the CEO of Medinex, a NASDAQ-listed electronic medical record (EMR) software company. I also helped pioneer the field of retail healthcare as I built up my current company, iRemedy, to be the "Amazon of healthcare." I have participated in panel discussions at the Naval War College and have advised and consulted with the leaders of hundreds of healthcare and insurance companies. I've also worked with governors, senators, and other public officials and their staffs, and have been a candidate for the U.S. House of Representatives. This experience has deepened my understanding of the challenges (and opportunities) that exist in U.S. healthcare and the medical supply chain.

During the forty years since I left Michigan, the slow degradation of the U.S. manufacturing base has continued unabated. Globalization has led to the offshoring of our supply chain, manufacturing, jobs, technology, and manufacturing expertise. Jobs, technology, and raw material mining have moved overseas, sometimes to countries that encourage slave labor, give polluters a free pass to trash the environment, and have no interest in the prosperity or security of the American people.

Today, Flint, once the epicenter of postwar American prosperity, is synonymous with Rust Belt decay. It is downright tragic. Name any kind of social or economic dysfunction (unemployment, drug abuse, infrastructural degradation, mass incarceration), and chances are, it exists in Flint. On a recent visit to my hometown, my wife and I drove by the house where my parents raised me and my three brothers. It was for sale—for $12,000.

The loss of jobs and economic livelihood is in and of itself devastating. But when globalization means that something as essential as medical supplies is offshored, the problem takes on greater urgency.

When the pandemic was upon us, our weak supply chain became a full-fledged life-or-death disaster.

The employees at my company, iRemedy, are experts in medical supply sourcing and have built an artificial intelligence technology that was designed to manage the needs of the thousands of healthcare providers we serve. So we were well suited to play a central role as the importer of over a billion medical items that were essential to our nation's response to COVID-19. In the process, we had bad agents around the world try to steal our products and rob us of millions of dollars, and we found ourselves in the diplomatic crossfire between the White House, the Department of Defense, the Chinese Communist Party, and a network of Chinese manufacturers.

The link between the decline of U.S. manufacturing on one hand, and public health on the other, is plainly visible: our reliance on foreign sources—particularly an antagonistic, anti-American China—for drugs and medical equipment puts us all at great risk, while emboldening and enriching an adversary. China has such a firm grip on the supply chain that Beijing could injure or even kill millions of Americans without firing a shot. And we have no defense.

Medicine and medical supply is therefore not just a public health issue; it's a matter of national security. The story in this book lays bare that fact, hopefully enough to shock the nation into action.

My son Anthony has been part of this journey as he fulfilled his role as a leader at our company. If my father's generation built the greatest economy in the history of the world, and my generation witnessed its unraveling, I wonder what kind of world Anthony will inherit. Will we resolve to fix the problem—or will we simply slog onward on a long, slow decline, twiddling our thumbs until the next, even deadlier health crisis befalls us?

CHAPTER 1

AN UNSEEN THREAT

A thirty-five-year-old Seattle-area man settles into seat 23F, coughs once, and closes his eyes to the quiet disorder of the preflight routine: flight attendants shuffling up and down the aisle, passengers cramming their carry-ons into the hold, the click of seatbelts, the sighs of travelers about to embark on a long, trans-Pacific flight—China to Washington state.

After a pleasant few days visiting family in Wuhan, Mr. 23F is feeling a little under the weather. No one, least of all him, knows that the SARS-CoV-19 virus is rapidly multiplying inside his body.[1] In twelve hours, he'll touch down at Seattle-Tacoma International Airport, marking the terminus of his journey—but just the start of the coronavirus's coast-to-coast tour as it makes its debut in the United States, en route to changing history forever.

At this point in January 2020, COVID-19 had been reported in the press, but mostly as a marginal, beneath-the-fold story or brief international news item buried on page twelve. It was, so we thought, far from our shores; hardly the cataclysmic, unprecedented event it would soon blow up into. The disease had escaped the borders of China, where it originated, but few public health officials anywhere were predicting that it would soon undertake a world tour, swamping the health systems of Italy, the UK, the U.S., and many other nations within a month.

Around the time that the man soon to be identified as America's COVID patient zero[2] was scrolling through the in-flight movie listings, I was huddled in a glass-walled conference room in a Manhattan office building, meeting with my company's board of directors. iRemedy, where I serve as founder and CEO, operates the nation's largest online marketplace for health and medical supplies. We are the go-to source for retail consumers, healthcare providers, and government agencies. That day, the words "COVID," "pandemic," or "vaccine" were not on the agenda. It was business as usual. Or so we thought.

Mid-meeting, a call came in from Amanda Somsy, our CFO in Florida. If she was calling during a board meeting, I knew it had to be important.

"Hi Amanda, you're on speaker phone. What's up?" I said.

"Sorry to interrupt, but something unusual is going on. I thought you should know."

She proceeded to report that in recent days, our company had received a sudden influx of orders for face masks and gloves, placed by thousands of people all around the country. Based on their names and addresses, they seemed to be civilians rather than the healthcare professionals we usually serve. While we do provide supplies to individual consumers, this sudden spike was anomalous.

"There's something else weird about it," she said. "Almost all of these customers have Chinese names."

That is, of course, not a problem in and of itself, but in e-commerce you're extra-sensitive about any kind of unusual sales patterns, since they are often an indicator of fraud. It was something we dealt with regularly, in fact; part and parcel of e-commerce, unfortunately. Usually the scammer will place a big order with a stolen credit card, and by the time we get wise to it, the shipment has already been delivered and there's little we can do to retrieve it. Or they simply dispute the charge and get a refund from the credit card company, then turn around and ship the fraudulently obtained product overseas or to another complicit party, at which point it's sold on the gray market.

In order to combat this, we use sophisticated fraud detection software to ferret out suspicious patterns. The software provider underwrites the risk, so as long as a purchase passes the software's test, they absorb the cost. That frees us of the burden of playing detective to determine whether any given order is phony or not.

"Did it pass our fraud software?" I asked.

"Yes."

"Well, then keep shipping them out." It was indeed strange—people usually aren't clamoring for masks and gloves, but if the software said it was legitimate, we were safe.

As one of the few medical supply providers open to the public, we occupy a unique position in the healthcare landscape; our business is sensitive to the vagaries of public health. We are the canary in the coal mine. And the spike in orders by Chinese customers was a sign that something big was coming. But even we had no idea of the tsunami that was rapidly approaching.

In the weeks that followed that January board meeting, the anomalous ordering of masks and gloves by persons with Chinese names kept rolling in, and our PPE inventory was quickly depleted. First, the last boxes were pulled from the shelves of our twenty-five-thousand-square-foot warehouse in Florida. Our other warehouses in Chicago and Houston followed suit. We started buying out our suppliers—and then they started running out too.

Our whole business model, and a big reason we're an industry leader—the Amazon of medical supplies, if you will—is attributable to a finely honed, AI-powered system of anticipating shortages and filling needs, whatever, wherever, whenever. It's what we do best. If you're a doctor or a hospital administrator or just an ordinary citizen with medical needs, and you need something that for some reason you can't find anywhere else, we excel at getting it to you. In fact, we were discussing improvements to our AI system the very moment Amanda's urgent phone call came in.

Most people don't want shortages. We, on the other hand, want to know about a product no one has, because that identifies to us an opportunity. Although shortages are endemic to the healthcare system, they usually are short-lived and manageable. Except in rare cases, no one dies as a result.

That was all about to change, because as COVID ravaged the world, causing sudden and unforeseen demand for pretty much every medical item in the catalogue, every doctor, nurse, clinic, hospital, ER, and surgical center in the United States was scrambling to secure a limited supply.

Whether it was for drugs, ventilators, protective equipment, or needles and syringes, every link in the chain of production was being squeezed. Something insidious was unfolding in the early months of 2020. And it cruelly exposed long-standing vulnerabilities in the medical supply system we had blithely come to assume would always remain functioning. Decades of globalization and outsourcing of production had made us susceptible to a crisis like the one coronavirus was about to present. Before COVID, few sounded the alarm, but now it had become painfully clear: it was only a matter of time before mass shortages turned from an occasional inconvenience to a literal matter of life and death.

And the system remains flawed—another powder keg waiting for the next spark.

This is not a book about the pandemic, or about the healthcare system's response to it, or our government's far-reaching and sometimes controversial efforts to contain the virus and encourage—or in some cases, mandate—vaccinations and treatments. Those events form part of the story, for we were deeply involved in the race to get America vaccinated, but this book is about something bigger. For even as COVID-19 has waned, populations have become inoculated, and masks have been thrown in drawers or relegated to a pocket of that coat you haven't worn since the long winter of 2021, the pandemic exposed dangerous fractures and fissures in a globalized healthcare system and transnational supply network that once seemed impervious but which is actually perilously brittle—placing all of us at risk as a result.

It's a book about how virtually every medically-related "thing"—from the over-the-counter painkillers you take for a headache, to sophisticated prescription drugs, to the diaphragm in a stethoscope, to the microchips in a MRI scanner, to the metals used to manufacture wheelchairs and crutches—is sourced and produced overseas, in nations with tenuous, or even antagonistic, relations with the United States. The greatest of these is China, a geopolitical rival to which we are completely beholden when it comes to producing the stuff we depend on for our physical health. Contrary to the story we Americans like to tell about ourselves—that our nation is robust and self-reliant—we are an anemic, bedridden patient entirely dependent on distant "caregivers" whose priority is their own well-being, not ours. China and other countries are the arbiters of a globalized supply chain system that, despite the appearance of stalwart reliability, can break down at any moment, for any number of reasons. Pandemics are one such reason. Armed conflict, diplomatic hostilities, trade wars, and other forms of geopolitical strife are also an ever-present threat. The medical supply system isn't just "at risk;" it can be weaponized to further the aims of a hostile power. And we have little recourse if that occurs.

Race against the Clock

The run on personal protective equipment (PPE) that iRemedy experienced in January and February 2020 was a harbinger of a much bigger battle into which our company would soon be thrust.

By summer 2020, the virus was out of control. Infection rates had gone up exponentially, and the growing multitude of patients, some seriously ill, severely strained the medical supply system, a crisis visibly and memorably illustrated in the tragicomic tableau of nurses and doctors wrapping themselves with trash bags once their reserve of masks, gloves, and booties started running out. But it wasn't just gloves and masks. There were shortages of basically everything, everywhere, putting healthcare workers and patients alike at risk.

And the U.S. simply does not have the domestic manufacturing capability to make what is needed when foreign imports cease. That is true even in the best of times.

At iRemedy, we were trying to keep pace with the demand, filling an increased volume of orders while also meeting the regular health needs of our customers for non-coronavirus related care. We're a small company with just twenty employees, but we kept doing what we do best. We never shut down. But it was a daily, herculean struggle. In our line of work, we never forget the stakes: when you don't deliver, people die.

There was, however, a silver lining amidst this crisis: by summer, researchers were already making great strides toward developing an effective vaccine, even if no one knew exactly when it would be ready to be deployed, nor how to overcome the logistical challenges of inoculating billions of people. This vaccine would face its own challenges and controversies as its development and deployment were swept up in a broader government effort to battle COVID. We stayed out of that debate and focused on our mission. For us, it was clear that thousands of our healthcare provider clients, and millions of high-risk patients, needed and wanted the vaccine. It was no exaggeration to say that the fate of the nation, and really the world, hung on getting these people their shot in the arm.

And then, with one phone call, we were parachuted onto the front lines of the war against COVID.

In August 2020, Anthony Paquin, our VP of government sales and supply chain, was working from his office overlooking Times Square when the phone rang. It was Phil Clayton, the president of Goldbelt Security, a subsidiary of Goldbelt Inc., an

Alaskan Native Corporation that procures products and services for the federal government, fulfilling several hundred million dollars in federal contracts each year.

Phil Clayton is a retired Green Beret, a former sergeant major, and a grizzled old Special Forces type. He's also the spitting image of Donald Sutherland playing President Snow in *The Hunger Games* films.

That day, Phil had a strange request. "I've called sixty-three distributors and basically everyone hung up on me. I'm looking for needles and syringes. A *lot.*"

"How many is 'a lot'?" said Anthony.

"One hundred million."

"*How* much?"

"The federal government needs a hundred million."

That was a staggering number, much larger than any order we had ever processed (and probably larger than our competitors had handled, either). But with the first batch of vaccines expected to be rolled out later that year, the public would need every one of those needles. It was a critical part of Operation Warp Speed, the U.S. government's massive private-public campaign to expedite COVID vaccine development and inoculate every American who wanted immunity against the virus.

Anthony said that we could do it. If not us, who?

"You're the first person to even have a conversation with me. Everyone else laughed me off the phone," said Phil. He had been calling suppliers around the country in a desperate attempt to source the product. They had all dismissed him with variations of, "Look, we're just trying to keep the lights on here. Forget providing a hundred million of anything."

As soon as he got off the phone with Goldbelt, Anthony called me up. I was at home in Florida, drinking a cocktail on the lanai. He relayed the conversation he'd had with Phil. Needless to say, I was as startled as Anthony.

"Yeah, with all the talk of vaccines," I said, "I hadn't thought about how they were going to deliver them."

"Neither had I. No one is talking about it. This is a problem," said Anthony.

"Or an opportunity. How many are they looking for?"

"One hundred million."

"One hundred million! Jesus. Can we even get them?"

"No. Nothing's available."

"What did you tell him?"

"I told him we can do it."

"Well, damn," I said. "Let's figure it out then. Someone's gotta be able to do it. If we don't have needles, we don't have a vaccine."

Then I pulled out a notepad and we got to work. A hundred million needles and syringes means a *million* boxes, each about the size of a VHS tape. That started putting things in perspective.

Fortunately, because of the way our technology platform works, we had a better sense than anyone of where the needles were being made, and in which factories, since they are all preapproved by the FDA. This is publicly available data, but no one else was tracking it. And we had key relationships with these overseas producers. Of course they, too, were struggling with the pandemic, but we were confident that one way or another, we could get what we needed.

"One other thing," said Anthony, who had clearly buried the lede. "Phil says the government requires that they're all made in America or ally nations."

Large procurement contracts like these are often managed on behalf of the government by the Department of Defense (DoD). They are experts in "buying stuff," as Phil explained, and were the only government institution that could muster the operational resources to manage a large project like this. When there is an urgent need for a large procurement contract, even one that has no military bearing, the federal government turns to the DoD to manage it, as they are the government experts in buying and moving large amounts of stuff, including medical supplies.

The DoD is (understandably) demanding, and, as we were soon to discover, the contract would be the most difficult any of us had ever fulfilled. But the contract officers were fair, professional, and mission-driven, doing what they felt was best for their country (even if working with them sometimes caused consternation).

Unfortunately, it would be impossible to comply with their request to produce all the needles and syringes in the United States or a friendly nation. While no one really knows exactly how many needles and syringes are domestically produced, it's a small fraction of the total annual usage. Becton Dickinson (BD) is one major American needle manufacturer but they wouldn't even be in the ballpark with this kind of volume. The vast majority, including BD's, are made abroad.

And therein lay the problem: even something as essential and simple as a syringe had been outsourced. The fact that the federal government agents even *thought* the domestic capacity existed showed how blithe they (and basically all of us) had become, how oblivious to the extent of our foreign dependence we all were. When America desperately needed a big supply, it had no recourse except to look east. And our small company had been given a mission that evidently no one else could achieve.

That federal order—the biggest single order for needles and syringes in history—was just the start of a byzantine odyssey that forced us to deal with cutthroat factory owners, shady middlemen, dubious profiteers, fraudsters, and scammers, along with the Chinese Communist Party itself, in a race against the clock to bring vital supplies to the American public in the face of an unprecedented health catastrophe that by mid-2020 was picking off thousands of victims each day.

Through it all, we learned the dangerous, if not deadly, threat posed by our reliance on Chinese and other foreign sources to keep the healthcare system functioning.

COVID put the globalization of healthcare, and all its inherent risks and shortcomings, into focus and created the opportunity to examine the problems involved in each step of the medical supply chain—while serving as a warning that it could happen again, unless we find a solution.

The Globalization of Healthcare: A Double-Edged Sword

Economic globalization has tethered far-flung nations together in an intricate system of interdependence. This development has contributed to torrid economic growth that has benefited both developed and developing nations alike. Many of us in the United States have enjoyed tremendous advantages as a result. American consumers benefit from cheap overseas goods that are quickly available; American companies thrive on low-cost labor and the unfettered flow of capital across borders. On the other side of the equation, once-impoverished nation-states like China and India have grown into economic powerhouses thanks to access to lucrative foreign markets in Europe, Africa, and North and South America. The economic marriage of convenience between west and east, and between global north and global south, has given rise to thriving manufacturing sectors in China and elsewhere that churn out all manner of goods—including medical supplies—as they feed the insatiable demand of Western consumers.

Globalization is why in the dead of winter, a German schoolteacher tucking into breakfast can enjoy fresh strawberries (grown in the south of Spain), or a Canadian teenager can afford the latest model of smartphone by Samsung (a Korean company that manufactures its devices in Vietnam before shipping them off to Vancouver). Or why pharmaceutical companies can synthesize hundreds of vital, life-sustaining drugs in Chinese factories at low cost and send them across the sea by the container-load so that our drugstores and hospital shelves are stocked with what we need when we need it.

This vast and intricate web of production and consumption is held together by supply chains that move goods from one end of the earth to the other, 24/7/365. Just take a look at the real-time map of container ships at VesselFinder.com—a cavalcade of little colored dots on a field of blue—to get a sense of the scale of it. They look like worker ants scurrying around a vast colony, crisscrossing the planet in a ceaseless and manic frenzy of commerce. There's no doubt that globalization has produced losers as well as winners, and some have benefited more—much more—than others, but generally, the latter outnumber the former. We've all grown accustomed, if not addicted to, the benefits of cheap, fast, and efficient.

The thing with this system is that it works well—until it doesn't. And when COVID hit, workers were out sick or confined to isolation, ships and planes stopped moving, and supply lines ruptured. Countries that had been "economic partners" suddenly put their own healthcare interests first, everyone else be damned. Suddenly "we're all doing business together" devolved into "every man for himself."

And just like that, China, the dependable, always-there engine of production and export that American healthcare administrators, physicians, and patients have unwittingly come to rely on for everything from antibiotics to high-tech medical devices to diagnostic tests to first aid kits to surgical masks and gauze, could not be counted on to produce and ship those items. And our own healthcare system does not stock these vital products in large quantities. Indeed, this very system of globalization has obviated the need for amassing inventory in favor of a highly efficient, low-cost, "just in time" model—which, again, worked until it didn't.

We were caught flat-footed. And it's only a matter of time before another crisis causes the same shortages. What if, God forbid, the next time it's worse?

Our dependence on foreign states, and especially China, puts all of us at grave risk. Perhaps we will never endure another pandemic that brings supply chains to a grinding, deadly halt. But any number of other contingencies could emerge. As an emerging superpower, China is well aware of Western dependence on its factories, seaports, container ships, and labor force for the goods that power daily life.

Hence, the medical supply system is emerging as a "hidden front" in the increasingly acrimonious contest for global supremacy between China and the United States. Pundits tend to focus on the military realm, or the battle for economic predominance, or the technological arms race between Beijing and Washington. But control of the medical supply chain, from raw materials to manufacturing to logistics to shipping and transport, is another lever of power that the "Red Dragon" can use to project its might into the homes, hospitals, clinics, and medicine cabinets of ordinary Americans.

The two countries have benefited from a decades-long economic partnership, but underlying China's growth is a plan for global hegemony in which the aspirin on your drugstore shelves—or you—might be the next casualty.

We face a dire situation, and no one—not Washington, not the healthcare system, not patient advocacy groups or physicians—has a plan to fix it. But there is hope, as long as we muster the political and economic will to change. This book serves not only to sound the alarm, but also, based on my decades of experience in healthcare and as the leader of a cutting-edge company that played a pivotal role in helping deliver the COVID vaccine, to propose a solution. But we must act fast. If not, the pandemic will prove to be just the opening act in an even more cataclysmic tragedy in which our healthcare system falls apart.

CHAPTER 2

WHO MAKES THE STUFF IN YOUR MEDICINE CABINET

Open your medicine cabinet. What do you see? Tylenol. Claritin. A couple translucent orange vials containing prescription blood thinner or cholesterol meds. A half-used bottle of expired Percocet from that wisdom tooth surgery six years ago, which you remind yourself you really need to get around to disposing of.

The medicines we and our loved ones take each day are life-improving, life-sustaining, and in some cases even life-giving. Their absence could be devastating, but usually (at least for the properly insured), the only thing that separates us from the pills we need is a fifteen-minute wait at the CVS pharmacy counter. From ordinary over-the-counter medication that eases cold symptoms or soothes aching muscles, to complex and critical Rx drugs that keep us healthy and alive, we tend not to second-guess their availability or wonder about their provenance.

We can hardly fathom a world where these drugs would be unobtainable. Nor do we really ask who makes them, where they come from, or how they get from the manufacturer to the distributor to the retailer to your nightstand. If you're taking, say, Pravachol to regulate your cholesterol, you don't care where it's made or how, as long as it works and it's there when you need it.

However, the reliability and ease of access to medications obscures the fact that most of those pills are made of raw materials sourced thousands of miles from home, in China, India, Russia, and elsewhere. And it's not just medication—virtually all of the medical equipment that physicians, nurses, radiologists, and lab technicians rely on to measure, medicate, maintain, and manipulate patient health depends on raw materials that are foreign-sourced.

Even if we had the manufacturing capability needed to make these supplies, we would not have access to the basic components and raw materials. It is no exaggeration to say that the beating heart, the breathing lungs, and the muscles and tissues of our "body politic" depend entirely on access to such materials. Our dependency on foreign powers goes all the way back to the beginning of the process.

Active Pharmaceutical Ingredients (APIs)

Few people have heard of the term "active pharmaceutical ingredients," or APIs, but virtually everyone will depend on them at some point for their physical well-being if not their continued survival. Probably you've got some acetylsalicylic acid in your medicine cabinet right now—that's the API in aspirin, used also in pills that treat pain, stroke, cardiovascular problems, and other maladies.

Like the flour, sugar, or yeast in your pantry, APIs are the building blocks for making a drug. They're lab-synthesized chemical compounds, usually in powder form, that are vital for creating a range of substances, from the most common OTC products to the most obscure and complex medications.

Every drug has at least one API. Without APIs, you can't make pharmaceuticals, any more than you could bake a cake without flour or yeast.

The U.S. is critically dependent on foreign sources for its APIs, particularly—you guessed it—India and China. In fact, 80 percent of APIs for essential drugs consumed in the United States have no domestic source.[3] This wasn't always the case. America used to make most of the APIs that would eventually find their way into the bodies of its citizens, but, following the pattern in other industries, production moved offshore—particularly eastward.

Starting around twenty years ago, Chinese manufacturers started grabbing a bigger slice of the lucrative drug-market pie, and American and European drug companies, lured by China's lower production costs, were happy to oblige. Cheap labor and a well-developed business ecosystem of manufacturers, distributors, and suppliers made for a more attractive environment to produce APIs.

Moreover, China's permissive regulatory environment provided another advantage. API production can be a dirty business, involving a panoply of toxic chemicals harmful to both human and environmental health. Overseas manufacture allowed drug companies to circumvent regulations at home that make domestic manufacture more complex and costly.[4]

After a few decades of offshoring, the geography of API production looks nothing like it did before. Today, 86 percent of the global supply of tetracycline and doxycycline (vital antibiotics) is made in China, as is 63 percent of Vitamin B1 and nearly half of all aspirin.[5] Acetaminophen, hepatin (a blood anticoagulant), amoxicillin (another antibiotic), and valsaratan (a blood pressure medication) are also predominantly made in China.[6] In 2018, "China accounted for 95 percent of U.S. imports of ibuprofen, 91 percent of U.S. imports of hydrocortisone [and] 40 to 45 percent of U.S. imports of penicillin."[7]

But India is giving China a run for its money and has emerged as a pharmaceutical powerhouse. According to research by U.S. Pharmacopeia, a nonprofit concerned with the medical supply chain, India has the most factories in the world that produce more than ten active ingredients for the U.S. market, with 183 such factories housed in the subcontinent (eighty-three are in Europe; thirty-five are located in China).[8] Furthermore, India accounts for 48 percent of active API Drug Master Files (DMF). A DMF is a document that details a drug product's manufacture, purity, stability, and origin, among other data. China makes up 13 percent and Europe 22 percent of API DMFs, while the U.S. accounts for just one-tenth. [9]

However, India's apparent advantage over China in API production obscures another unsettling truth: that China still controls the materials used to make APIs, which are themselves composed of "key starting materials (KSMs)" and "intermediates"—simple chemical substances. If APIs are the building blocks, KSMs and intermediates are the wood the blocks are made out of. So while India accounts for 20 percent of global generic drug production by volume, 70 percent of the APIs it uses for production are imported from China.[10]

Certainly, the offshoring of API production has been an economic boon to drug companies, but at what price? The cost is to both the companies themselves, which are now reliant on

China and India as suppliers, and to the American public at large, which has no idea that the origin of many of the substances they need to live and thrive are sourced halfway around the world, in one of two emergent, often unfriendly superpowers, each with its own geopolitical agendas and domestic priorities.

"Open more factories at home!" is the usual policy response to this situation, but that's more of a campaign slogan than a viable solution. It's not enough to simply start "making drugs" stateside, because as long as the raw materials for those drugs come from China, India, or elsewhere, we are still dependent on those countries.

The U.S. government stockpiles "essential" drugs, but if production or export in China or India ceased—whether by circumstance or, more sinisterly, by design—the U.S. would run out of medicine in a couple of weeks or months.[11] After COVID, we now understand that such disruptions are not merely a remote possibility. It happened before, and it could happen again. For example, in the early days of the pandemic, India imposed a moratorium on exports of acetaminophen and certain antibiotics to ensure ample domestic supply for its 1.3 billion citizens.[12] Americans are one foreign state's edict away from facing mass shortages of the drugs we blithely assume will be accessible wherever, whenever. And we are dangerously unprepared.

Microchips

Microchips, those little black silicon wafers that invisibly power virtually every facet of our technologically advanced life, are another weak link in the chain. The "technologization" of consumer products that a generation ago were pretty unsophisticated now means that even your toaster or electric toothbrush has a simple chip inside it.

Healthcare has also gone high-tech as sophisticated digital gadgetry has replaced its analog or mechanical predecessors, while creating an exciting new range of cutting-edge machines the likes of which doctors could only dream of a generation ago. For example, implantable drug delivery systems use microchips to keep track of physiological markers while automatically dispensing the needed dosage of medicine as you go about your day. Consider something like glucose monitors. It used to be that to check your blood sugar, you'd prick your finger and put a drop of blood on a special paper that would change color. Then that advanced to a simple device that would display a numerical reading. But today most glucose monitors are permanently attached to the body and just monitor constantly, in real time. No more uncomfortable finger poking.

The tiniest devices can perform a range of functions automatically, with pinpoint precision and flawless reliability. Implantable devices using microchips are an exciting frontier of medical technology, and their use is likely to dramatically increase. According to the article *Microchips in Medicine: Current and Future Applications*, "Advancements will allow expansion of this technology into a larger range of therapeutic areas. Drugs with dose delivery systems which would otherwise be considered difficult or undesirable could take place in passive manners. Treatments for diseases such as diabetes and hypertension where dose titrations are necessary could be revolutionized to create automated therapy regimens that are safer and more efficacious."[13]

Robotics is another branch of med-tech that is likely to be the next big thing, such as the DaVinci Surgical System, a bot that performs minimally invasive surgery with humanlike dexterity.

The future is now. But these state-of-the-art technologies need semiconductors to run. So do the panoply of more familiar, yet indispensable, devices used in everyday medical care, such as X-ray machines, MRI machines, CT scanners, ventilators, and heart rate monitors.

The advancement of med-tech is great for patients and doctors. But it further entrenches medicine in a state of digital dependency, because computer chips, and the raw materials they're made of, are largely sourced on foreign shores.

In 1990, the U.S. produced around 40 percent of semiconductors worldwide; Europe made another 40 percent. China was just a bit player in the microchip industry. You can surmise what happened next. As the semiconductor industry in Asia grew—facilitated by lower manufacturing costs—the U.S. lost market share as production in Japan, South Korea, Taiwan, and China exploded.[14] Today, Taiwan is the dominant producer. China accounts for 15 percent of global production, lagging behind Taiwan. But the precarious situation of Taiwan, a quasi-independent island nation that China claims as its own, places its globally vital microchip industry within the clutches of the PRC's increasingly hegemonic leaders. We'll study this issue later in the book, but even if China doesn't take the twenty-three-million-person island by force, it could strangle chip exports with a naval blockade, or deploy a number of other mechanisms to deny the U.S. and the rest of the world the semiconductors we all need to keep our glucose pumps pumping, our ventilators providing oxygen, and our imaging technologies detecting broken bones, cancer, and other maladies.

In truth, we don't actually need to speculate about the impact of a black swan event like Sino-American conflict—there's a major chip shortage happening at the time of this writing!

For the past few years, burgeoning demand has put a squeeze on global supply, exacerbated by COVID, contentious China-U.S. trade policies, and disruptive weather events. Given the ubiquity of integrated circuits in virtually every industry and facet of life, the shortage has had wide-ranging effects, and healthcare has not been spared. For example, representatives of companies that provide mammography, cancer scanning,[15] pacemakers, and brain scanning imagery[16] have struggled to provide services amidst a worldwide microchip shortage. As an executive of a company that produces breathing aids told the *Wall Street Journal*, "Every single chip [semiconductor suppliers] gives the gift of breath to a person suffocating."[17] Your life could depend on the availability of a one inch-by-one inch silicon square.

An additional challenge for manufacturers of medical devices is that their industry is relatively small compared to other industries whose products also rely on chips, which means that with many suppliers bidding on a limited supply, healthcare device companies could be marginalized. And one of the problems in healthcare, unlike other industries, is that the parts in high-tech devices are minimally interchangeable and thus you can't swap out suppliers as easily.

Say I'm making a type of monitor for a line of personal computers, and my usual microchip supplier suddenly goes under or has to halt production. Well, no chips, no monitors. My own company's output would grind to a halt. But the problem could be managed. It might take a few weeks or months to locate a substitute supplier, and my bottom line would probably take a hit, but I could weather the rough patch and carry on. And even the most ardent gamers or computer nerds wouldn't die if they couldn't buy one of my monitors.

But when you build a medical device around a particular chip, you're "locked into" that chip, which might have a single supplier, likely in China or Taiwan. If you lose access, then that's it.

With healthcare products, there's much more at stake; often, a supply shortage is literally a matter of life or death. There's also a complex and opaque regulatory landscape to navigate when it comes to producing healthcare devices that reflects the higher stakes. So if your key supplier of a particular chip you need goes belly up—or the nation-state where it operates bans exports, or war breaks out, or the next pandemic throws supply networks into disarray, or any number of plausible contingencies occurs—then people suffer and die. The relative complexity, precision, and obscurity of healthcare products injects variables into your processes that make production more delicate.

Even something as banal as medical records rely, ultimately, on computing and hence on microchips. Healthcare is a paperwork-heavy field, as anyone knows who has had to fill out seventeen different forms before a routine physical. Digitizing medical records was a huge breakthrough in healthcare in America because it freed us from the onus of keeping paper records. But like any technological advance, it's a double-edged sword: the computerization of medical records in vast digital databases also means that we no longer file by hand or keep paper backups. (It also created new opportunities for hackers, cyber warriors, and other malicious actors to pilfer, expose, tamper with, or hold for ransom private medical data).

The point is that without microchips, healthcare would grind to a halt. Medical professionals rely on digital technology for everything from checking a patient's blood pressure to conducting arthroscopic surgery. Once you go digital, you can't go back to analog.

Rare Earth Commodities

Rare earth elements are vital materials used in a host of functions, including industrial, chemical, technological, and consumer goods. They constitute one of the two lower rows of the periodic table: the fifteen "lanthanides" plus two others. With multisyllabic, exotic names like samarium, gadolinium, and terbium, they sound like made-up alien elements in a sci-fi novel, but while you may not recognize them by name, you likely use products that are built with rare earth materials every day. And they're absolutely essential to the medical system.

LED screens, GPS receivers, RF generators, permanent magnets (like the type used in MRI machines), laser technologies, hearing aid speakers—these high-tech medical gadgets cannot be built without rare earth metals.[18] Many of these technologies are built in America. But their material origin is more likely some mine in Inner Mongolia or the Congo. The heart monitor keeping Grandma alive after her operation? It starts with some Chinese guy blasting rock apart in an open pit in some barren and forsaken place halfway around the world.

As with APIs, the U.S. and a few other nations used to run the show, but China started eclipsing its competitors in raw material mining and processing around twenty years ago. The rapid growth of its mining industry has allowed China to vault ahead as the dominant source of these vital elements. Today, China supplies 45 percent of the world's critical raw materials—putting it far ahead any other nation, including the United States, which accounts for just 7 percent.[19]

India and Russia are also active participants in the rare earth game, but neither has the reserves or the productive capacity of the People's Republic. Vietnam and Brazil also hold vast reserves, but their extractive industries are likewise less developed, giving China a clear competitive advantage.

And like a glamorous woman turning heads as she struts across the dance floor at a swanky club, China knows what it's got and is not afraid to flaunt it. Its advantage in this area did not emerge by accident. Rather, it is a plank in a long-term strategy for global hegemony—something I'll examine further in the chapters to come. As far back as 1987, Deng Xiaoping, chairman of the Communist Party and "paramount leader" of the country, declared, "The Middle East has oil, China has rare earths."[20] As an incipient global power, China was in the late eighties a mere shadow of what it is today, but Deng's statement was a harbinger of things to come. It took China a few decades to establish pre-eminence in the rare earths industry, but there is no sign of reversing the trend, as Western nations are falling further behind each day.

Meanwhile, China has invested heavily in foreign mining operations, especially in Africa, extracting platinum, silicon, cobalt, and indium (the last of which is also used in semiconductor production), making the country "both the biggest producer of critical raw materials, but also the leading importer of those mined elsewhere."[21] What is doesn't own, it seeks to secure by some other means.

Part of the reason mining operations have shifted to China is because in the U.S., mining has a stigma (well-deserved, some would say). It's an "ugly" business that negatively affects both the environment and the health of its workers. However, as a nation, we did not eliminate our hunger for mined minerals; we merely outsourced their extraction. The "ugliness" persists; we just put it out of sight and out of mind.

While rare earth elements are to China what petroleum is to the Middle East—scarce, precious, geopolitically sensitive, and strategically invaluable—other, more common materials are also important to medical supplies. While they might not be "rare," their supply is still finite, and thus another locus of transnational competition, and a potential vulnerability to public health. For example, aluminum is normally not particularly rare, but a global aluminum shortage of the last few years has been a thorn in the side for manufacturers (and, by extension, consumers) of a range of products. Aluminum is widely used in health aids, such as crutches, wheelchairs, and walkers, and its dearth has had a direct impact on patients who rely on them every day.[22]

Nor would you think that something as relatively simple and low-tech as a needle or syringe would be hard to churn out, but a tight supply of both the plastic resin and the metals of which they are constructed has created some degree of scarcity for this most basic, indispensable, and widely used healthcare item.

In many cases, you can't easily shop around for a new supplier. A needle has a specific design, it must be made a certain way, it must be strong enough not to break, and its assembly requires the utmost precision, with specific parts. If you can't get the right raw materials, you can't make it.

Even in the best of times, there are shortages in the industry. This has been a vexing problem for a long time. At any given hospital, there are probably ten drugs that are low in stock (if not depleted entirely) and your job is to find alternative sources. If you don't, people suffer. People die.

One recent well-known example happened when Hurricane Maria knocked a factory out of commission in Puerto Rico. No one had previously realized that it was one of the few producers of IV fluid bags, which are about as widely used as nitrile gloves; it's hard to imagine running a hospital without them. After the hurricane, healthcare providers coast to coast experienced shortages. Virtually no one else in North America was making those bags.

The upheaval of COVID threw the precarity of the medical supply into sharp relief. That's when the cracks started to show.

We ran headlong into this scenario at the start of Operation Warp Speed. Once the government's unprecedented half-billion-count order for needles and syringes came through, we moved quickly to ramp up production.

Right away, raw materials became the bottleneck.

Once word got out that the U.S. government was moving to stockpile needles on a mass scale, others took notice worldwide. It was a scramble to see who could get it first. We at iRemedy had a jump on everyone else, but we had to move fast.

Securing the supply was not as simple as panic-buying the remaining stock of toilet paper at your local Costco, a scene that was meanwhile tragicomically playing out all over the country. You can't just load up the shopping cart and push it to the cashier. It involves a complex chain of sourcing, production, distribution, and sale twists and turns from the point of origin of the stuff needles and syringes are composed of, to the brokers and distributors, to health facilities that purchase them, to the patients on whom they are used. And most of the players in that chain are concentrated in, or doing business with, China.

When we tried to submit our orders for several hundred million needles and syringes, our factories in China were facing a squeeze too. They don't keep enough stainless steel, glass, and polymer lying around to produce that much. So right away the problem of production became a problem of raw material availability.

We were working with an intermediary broker (Northfield), based out of London, which purportedly had a direct line to the factories but, we later learned, was actually conducting business via a Hong Kong import export company (Tianjin Materials Company). Tianjin contracted with the factories to make the stuff, and they ultimately proved to be opportunistic, like many other brokers during the COVID pandemic.

One bottleneck was the nature of the product itself. Factories sprang up in China within ninety days to pump out the protective gear needed in hospitals worldwide. But a needle is a Class II medical device; it pierces the skin. It must be made with flawless precision and in accord with a bevy of health and safety regulations. Ramping up production is not so simple.

Fortunately for us, we went out and started locking up production contracts with the five biggest suppliers.

We spent day after day conducting frantic Zoom calls with our vendors, government contacts, import-export businesses, and contacts in China to get the ball rolling on production.

"Tony," said Paula, the Northfield executive who was our contact person, "if you want this order, they need a four-million-dollar deposit."

I was shocked. "Four million for what?"

"And they need it tomorrow."

Alarm bells clanged in my head. This was highly unusual. For one thing, I didn't know if we had the capital. And even if we did, that's a huge amount of cash to wire to China, basically on a wing and a prayer, without making sure the usual agreements are in place. And even if you *can* manage it, wiring funds to China takes a couple days, at best. It's complicated. It has to go through Hong Kong and a host of intermediary banks. There was no way we could do it in a day.

But they weren't budging. Four million or you can find someone else to produce your stuff, they told us flatly.

It didn't feel like business as usual. It felt like a shakedown.

But what could we do? If we didn't put down the deposit to allow the factories to secure the raw materials to produce the needles that a couple hundred million Americans were going to need to be vaccinated, someone else would: a hundred other companies, and countries, were breathing down our neck to get those raw materials too. And the factories and suppliers knew this. They had us between a rock and a hard place.

That was just one of a hundred problems we were about to face as COVID raged across the planet, supply chains broke down, and every conniving middleman from here to China sought to profit from the scarcity and capitalize on the chaos.

Asking the Right Questions

In my hand I'm holding a common household OTC medication. In tiny letters, next to the usual fine print about contraindications and proper dosage for children under twelve, is printed *MADE IN THE USA*. But I know there's more to the story than that; this product is not, in fact, made in the USA at all, but merely synthesized here, the final stop in a long chain that starts somewhere at a drab API manufacturing facility in Shandong Province or Mumbai, snakes across the Pacific, travels from a port to a pharma plant, and continues onward toward the clinic or drugstore down the street.

From simple items like vitamins, Tylenol, and weight scales, to more complex and life-giving devices like pacemakers, glucose monitors, and insulin pumps, they all are built by companies that need access to essential raw materials. The question we need to ask, therefore, is not "Who makes the stuff in your medicine cabinet or the devices in your hospital?" but "Who makes the stuff that is needed to make the stuff? And what happens if they stop making it or exporting it?"

The United States does not have a good answer to that question. And that imperils us all.

CHAPTER 3

THE SUPPLY CHAIN: ONLY AS STRONG AS ITS WEAKEST LINK

The last thirty to forty years of world trade have reshaped the global medical supply chain, giving rise to a vast, interlocking web of manufacturers, logistics specialists, raw material providers, inspectors, regulators, people involved in transport, export/import entities, payment processors, and others. It works well as long as there are no major bumps in the road. When it stops working, chaos ensues. That's exactly what happened during COVID, and pretty much the whole world was caught off-guard and unaware.

When you're talking about disruptions in the supply chain for, say, flatscreen TVs, the stakes are not as high. Sure, some people at various points in the chain are probably going to lose money, and someone's Super Bowl party might be ruined, but it's unlikely anyone is going to lose their life when the TVs don't get to the port, or to the wholesaler's warehouse, or to the Costco electronics aisle. When disruptions impact drugs and medical devices and masks and other life-sustaining products, the consequences are much graver. And when those disruptions occur during a global health emergency, when every aspect of the healthcare system—indeed, every facet of society in general—is already under strain, the effect is compounded.

How the Medical Supply Chain Works

In recent decades, supply chains for virtually every industry have transcended national borders; materials sourcing, production, and distribution all shifted to the worldwide stage. A global supply chain is multistage, complex, and dependent on the free flow of people and products around the world. People need to move to negotiate sourcing, manage logistics, and oversee production, and to perform the labor needed to transport crates of widgets from there to here, by truck, plane, and ship. Ironically, the same system of global trade that has been so efficient at production and distribution of vital goods also put everyone, from patients to physicians to hospital administrators, in a state of crisis, because when that system failed, there was no backup plan.

In our industry, before COVID, things mostly chugged along smoothly—business as usual. The network of government, healthcare providers (hospitals, doctors, etc.), distributors, logistics companies, global exporters, manufacturers, and raw material providers had settled into a system that generally worked smoothly. Shortages occurred, but the system was dynamic and efficient enough to plug any gaps before the dam burst. COVID threw all of that into disarray.

To understand why, let's examine how an average health establishment stocks what it needs to serve patients and protect doctors and nurses. Let's say you're the director of supplies at a hospital and you need a few hundred boxes of latex gloves.

Typically, those gloves would be manufactured in an authorized factory, one owned by a company whose name you do not know, in a remote Chinese city you've never heard of, and that's fine, because you don't order from the factory; you deal with a regional supplier who dealswith an even larger supplier who deals with some other intermediary (an import-export company). This continues all along the chain, back to the factory, where boxes of gloves fill up a case, and cases are loaded onto pallets, and those pallets are then loaded onto a truck, which then makes the long drive to a port like Shanghai or Shenzhen or Ningbo-Zhoushan.

Once the truck arrives, the pallets are loaded onto a 1,400-cubic-foot, 5,000-pound (empty) container, which is placed via crane onto a freighter (likely flying the flag of a country that is neither that of the origin nor the destination country) along with ten to twenty thousand other containers. The ship powers up its diesel engines and embarks on its long journey across the Pacific. That ship is one of hundreds if not thousands of freighters chugging around our blue planet at any given moment, each carrying untold quantities of clothing, kitchenware, appliances, fruits and vegetables, flowers, frozen seafood, power tools, radios and computers and tablets, auto parts—and of course, pills, medical electronics, PPE, and the like.

When the freighter reaches the west coast of the U.S., the containers are offloaded, the crates of latex gloves are loaded onto a truck, the driver makes the long haul to a warehouse, and from the warehouse, your boxes of gloves are dispatched until they arrive at your facility.

On and on and on, every week—a smoothly running commerce machine that linked sellers, buyers, and the many intermediaries who helped execute the exchange.

Though it was generally effective, even before COVID, there were risks and drawbacks to this system. One is that U.S. ports lag behind their European and Asian counterparts for automation and sophistication. Los Angeles and Long Beach rank last in the world for container efficiency.[23] Even under normal circumstances, we do a poor job importing and offloading the goods that are streaming in from abroad. Traffic jams at seaports slow offloading to a glacial pace. Most docks are unionized, so the threat of labor disputes and work stoppages, while infrequent, are ever-present.

Container shipping itself is for the most part a twentieth-century method that has been slow to adapt to twenty-first-century modes of technology and efficiency. Let's face it, containers are "dumb." It's not like Amazon where you can track your package at every step. Individual containers are not tracked in real time, nor do they utilize GPS; some aren't even climate-controlled. When you ship sophisticated medical equipment, you need to regulate the temperature and humidity on board, which limits your options for transoceanic transport.

And when those thousands of containers are flooding a port, searching for a shipment can be like looking for a needle in a haystack. It's difficult enough keeping track of which container is where at a given time. Moreover, these shipments are further hindered by inefficient movement from ship to dock to customs to the truck that takes them inland. The whole process is painfully slow—and maybe not the ideal way to get vital medicine and devices to where they're needed. But that's the system we must live with, at least for the foreseeable future.

The complex nature of medical supplies compounds the challenges of a global supply chain. Drawing on our hypothetical example, nitrile gloves are about as simple an item as it gets, but even those are subject to safety specifications; the FDA has a whole rule book governing the labeling, leak resistance, tear resistance, and biocompatibility of nitrile gloves. So you can imagine the detailed protocols in place for drugs and medical devices, which must be made to an exacting, ultraprecise standard. A single pill or ventilator might have to go through two dozen checks before it's approved. The slightest miscalibration can mean the difference between effective treatment or a fatal overdose. Anything that is going on, in, or connected to a human body will naturally require more stringent scrutiny.

Quality control adds extra hurdles to the process in various ways. Most drugs and devices are subject to "lot tracking": documenting what was made by which certified factory from which validated raw materials and under what quality testing, etc. In the factories we use for our needles and syringes, they keep a hundred units of every batch in a vault. If there's a malfunction or complaint, they can trace that exact item to that batch that is stored away. It's exhaustive—and, perhaps, exhausting. But it's par for the course. Playing fast and loose with safety and quality would put lives at risk. And even during a pandemic, one must still comply with those standards.

This also means that there is little flexibility when a particular device, or part of a device, you need suddenly becomes no longer available. In medicine, there is not the degree of interchangeability that exists in other product lines. If you're making radios and your circuit board supplier goes out of business, odds are you can source what you need from a dozen other suppliers. But it doesn't work this way in healthcare, where it's not uncommon for a single company to produce an essential part used in a device, or an essential chemical for synthesizing a drug. It's a major vulnerability. And in 2020, the entire global capacity for manufacturing needles was dependent on the output of one small injection mold supplier in China.

"Just in Time" in Times of Trouble

So during COVID when we stopped being able to import stuff from Asia, why couldn't we just tap into our reserve storage? That seems logical enough.

The short answer is that such reserves do not exist, at least not in adequate numbers. Not in federal facilities. Not in hospitals. Not in privately owned warehouses. Nowhere.

This is not an accident—not because some director of supplies abandoned their online shopping cart to go check their fantasy football team. It is by design.

One of the benefits of a frenetic, always-on-the-move system of global commerce is that generally, when you want it, you can get it. The regular, systematic production and delivery of goods, precisely calibrated to consumer need and fixed according to a predictable schedule, keeps the shelves stocked and the lights on. This is true of most industries, not just medical supplies.

It's a "just in time" strategy of supply that obviates the need for stockpiling large amounts of materials. A manufacturer might say, "We'll have it in stock for you. Call us when you need it." And the buyer says, "Great! I don't have to keep extra stock lying around." But the distributor—the intermediary between the manufacturer and the consumer—says, "We don't want six months of stock on hand either." So their logistics guy works out a plan that keeps goods flowing through the chain without having to hoard large quantities of anything. The logistics person says, "We have containers coming in each week, so you'll have some stock stateside and ten days' worth of stock floating across the Pacific, while our partner will meanwhile be making more inventory overseas."

In this system, everyone in the supply chain avoids the logistical onus and financial risk of keeping stock on hand.

Factories, containers, ships, airplanes, ports, trucking—all were coordinated to deliver that product when it was needed in the amount that was needed. And no more. That's the just-in-time model in action. Globalization compresses time and space. It doesn't matter if it originates in Shenzhen Province or Siberia—the answer is always, "we'll get it to you." The whole world has shifted toward this model.

In medicine, it's been a boon because it frees health facilities of the costly burden of storing a bunch of stuff in a warehouse. Think of the thousands of items used on a daily basis in hospitals: not just the disposable stuff, but the sophisticated gadgetry (and the spare parts needed to maintain it). Imagine the headaches involved in just *figuring out* how much of each item you're going to need for the year, much less actually finding the space to store it and the systems and human capital needed to maintain it.

And then you'd have to worry about expiration dates. Medical products don't last forever. Drugs expire. Chemicals degrade. Sometimes regulatory standards or best practices change and a drug or device becomes obsolete. Providing healthcare is challenging enough without having to worry about buying all the necessary supplies and warehousing them for years.

Instead, the globalized supply chain and its always-on, efficient transnational flow of goods has become our supply closet. Reach in and grab what you want. Yes, it takes a month for that container ship to cross the Pacific, but another one is arriving today, and more are on the way.

Another problem is that while the supply chain is generally efficient, it's relatively inelastic. You can't dramatically ramp up production on a whim, especially for sophisticated or high-precision items like diagnostic equipment, Rx drugs, or even (as we would come to learn) needles and syringes. While the length and complexity of the chain is a strength, it's also a weakness, because if you want to triple your output, or start churning out a new product, you have to go all the way back up the chain to the factory, the raw materials—everything. So that factory is already "programmed" to operate at a certain capacity. You want ten times more of X and you've got the cash? Certainly your supplier will do business with you. But it won't happen overnight. They'll have to build out another line, if not another plant.

Then you've got currency issues: currency fluctuations impact the buying and selling of goods. You need the same amount of raw materials, but your currency deflates, so you can't buy enough.

Everyone is trying to be cost-competitive. No one is making extra 'just in case' or building extra capacity.

Moreover, most healthcare institutions utilize an allocation-based system: present-year allocations are based on last-year usages. Yes, there is some flexibility to account for shifts in need, but only to a limited extent. Generally, especially in larger healthcare organizations, your department can only buy what you bought the previous year. You can imagine what occurs when this system, which is usually beneficial to all parties, runs up against a black swan event like a pandemic, and the need for basically everything increases dramatically.

Therefore, healthcare entities, instead of building up a reservoir of essential supplies, have focused on *reducing* the number of days of supply on hand, thanks to the cost involved in storing it. The less we have in stock, the better—as long as there is *some* in stock.

No one ever planned on this system being disrupted on a wide scale—which, since it can be disrupted for any number of reasons, was probably naïve. But no one working in healthcare had ever experienced an epidemic on the scale of COVID, and few had lived through a world war or the kind of international conflagration that could bring shipping to a standstill.

But then it happened.

What about the federal government? you might ask. Indeed, the government does maintain a "Strategic National Stockpile (SNS)" of essential health-related supplies, including PPE, medicine, and so forth. But the government, even with its virtually limitless resources, encounters the same problems as your neighborhood urgent healthcare clinic: products expire or become obsolete, and you need warehouses and people to maintain and keep track of them.

Thus, the SNS is engineered for health emergencies narrower in time and space, to safeguard against transitory events like an act of terrorism, not a nationwide (much less *global)* paucity of such basic things as surgical gowns or needles—and certainly not a public health crisis that drags on for months and years.

As Dan Gerstein, a former official in the Department of Homeland Security and a disaster response scholar, told *The Bulletin of the Atomic Scientists:*

> "We were always kind of talking about terrorism type events. And when you're thinking about a terrorism type event, you're probably not thinking a national event. . . . One of the things to happen is that, right away, your stockpile isn't scaled to meet a national event; it's scaled to meet maybe a series of localized events."[24]

Hence, the just-in-time system has yielded a curious situation of "abundant scarcity"—as long as that wheel of global commerce kept turning, whether you were an American middle-class shopper at Best Buy or a director of supplies at a major hospital, you could have what you wanted, when you wanted it. But that always-on availability was, we now understand, somewhat illusory.

The chain is only as strong as its weakest link. And when multiple links in the chain fail to bind, the whole structure falls apart.

When they do, it is unlikely that there's a backup plan or other recourse. Maybe you'll be lucky enough to find some other factory, some other shipping entity, some other logistics company that can plug the hole. But if you do, that ersatz solution is likely to be far from home, nowhere near America.

COVID obliterated the linchpins of that system, affecting offshore manufacturing, raw material availability, and global logistics systems. Because while it's easy to talk about "supply chains" in the abstract, every link in the chain involves people to mine, refine, process, fabricate, assemble, move, package, offload, unbox, and deliver the "stuff." The ripple effect of lockdowns and illness brought it all to a grinding halt. Suddenly, you couldn't move anything around the world.

As Vaclav Smil writes in *How the World Works*:

"The COVID-19 pandemic provided additional powerful arguments [against globalization] based on irrefutable concerns about the state's fundamental role in protecting the lives of its citizens. That role is hard to play when 70 percent of the world's rubber gloves are made in a single factory, and when similar or even higher shares of not just other pieces of PPE but also of principal drug components and common medications . . . come from a very small number of suppliers in China and India. Such dependence might fulfill an economist's dream of mass output at the lowest possible unit cost, but it makes for extremely irresponsible, if not criminal, governance."[25]

Subsequent geopolitical events with China and Russia have prolonged these problems—a reminder that even if we banish COVID to the history books, other disruptions can emerge. For example, as of this writing in 2022, exam tables, wheelchairs, crutches, and canes are backlogged in part because of the war in Ukraine, since Russia is a significant exporter of nickel, chrome, and steel. The cost for exam tables, for example, has soared by as much as 30 percent, with order wait times of four to five months.[26]

By summer 2020, the world was on fire. People were dying in droves. In July, sixty thousand new COVID cases were being reported daily in the U.S. By the end of the month, fourteen hundred people each day were losing their lives to the virus.[27]

One of my friends is head of emergency supply at a large hospital in New York City. I can't say which one, but it's probably one you've heard of even if you don't live in that particular city. This is a man who is not easily rattled. Twenty years toiling in the pressure cooker of overseeing the supply of a major medical establishment had given him nerves of steel. But when he called me one night on the verge of tears, it drove home how dire the situation had become.

"Our emergency team is wearing trash bags as gowns. I went downstairs to our supply closet to see how many we have left—and you know what I discovered? We don't even have a supply closet."

I assured him we'd do whatever possible to deliver what he needed. My next step was to call Anthony, who was already working our global supply network, and he spent the night pacing around his shoebox apartment while his girlfriend slept on the couch as he made call after call after call to contacts in China and Korea. Finally he found someone who could ship the gowns. It was a tiny victory in a war that we all felt we were losing.

And that was just one hospital in one city. Similar scenes were playing out in hospitals and clinics all over America and the world. Gowns. Masks. Ventilators. IV supplies. Cardiovascular drugs and other medicine. They weren't just scraping the barrel—there was no barrel to scrape.

It was clear that even if we could provide the healthcare system with the supplies they needed, the only way out of this global crisis was widespread inoculation. In summer 2020, researchers were making headway, but the first vaccines approved for the general public were months away. Regardless, no syringes meant no vaccine. The role of iRemedy in sourcing needles and syringes had grown, and with it, the importance of our mission.

They say that wars are won on logistics and supplies. When there's no food, blankets, and boots getting to the troops on the front line, the war effort crumbles. That was the kind of war we were fighting as the government made preparations to administer the vaccine that had yet to be approved: figuring out how to transport supplies to the front lines of the war while the pandemic rained down hellfire.

At iRemedy, our problem was twofold: not just delivering needles and syringes, but getting someone to make them first.

First, in order to kick-start production of this unprecedentedly large purchase order, we had no choice but to send four million dollars in cash deposits off into the ether; a "spray and pray" infusion of capital we hoped would be enough to grease the wheels of the shady network of Chinese factories, middlemen, and raw materials providers that we had to deal with. We took every precaution to be sure we would get our deposits back, and had only a dim understanding of where the money was going, but we had no choice. At least it kept us in business, and one step ahead of our competitors, who were angling to lock down the same raw material supply and manufacturing capacity needed for a few hundred million needles and syringes.

For the team at iRemedy, our lives became an unceasing cadence of daily Zoom meetings and frantic emails with our contacts in the UK and Asia—an exhausting dance across time zones and language gaps. That meant a lot of calls very late at night (morning in Beijing), often with people with little to no English language ability, requiring us to lean heavily on Google Translate to make ourselves understood. And then we had to navigate a byzantine network of quasi-private, quasi-public entities to get through to the right people. "Who really owns what?" is a big question when doing business with China. Sometimes that means you deal with a factory manager, sometimes the purported owner, sometimes local political officials or members of the party. It can be maddening.

Working this way was a comedy of errors that would have been amusing if not for the urgency of the work in the face of the virus's growing human toll.

Besides the frustration of bleary-eyed, Tower of Babel communications, the people on the other end, the ones we were doing business with, were also contending with the same fear, anxiety, and pestilence, which amplified the stress. They too were working in isolation, trying to keep themselves and their families heathy while contending with lockdowns, and slowdowns, and breakdowns in every industry, and disruptions to all facets of life.

Our problems compounded—as did the size of our commitments. As other vendors that had been hired by the government to procure needles and syringes folded or failed to execute on their agreements, our initial 100-million-needle order ballooned: first to 230 million, and later to 500 million.

We sat around the table, looked at each other, and realized, "Whoa. The federal government basically wants to buy up every needle in the world."

The unfathomable had grown impossible. But we had to find a way.

A worldwide scramble to secure billions of needles was underway: every country, and every vendor like us within those countries, was racing to fill their inventory. Our contract actually had the effect of amplifying this competition, once others got wind of it. When the U.S. government does something like this, they use an open bidding process. And when you call up a factory in China and discuss buying hundreds of millions of units, people talk. You can't really keep it under wraps.

We went back to Northfield and to our factory contacts in China and asked them to ramp up production even further. Additional demands for seven-figure deposits ensued (accompanied by threats to cut ties with us and keep the deposits we already sent if we delayed additional payments), further squeezing our finances and elevating the financial risk. In such times, finances take a back seat to the life and death mission of helping people, but we still had to keep the company running. Our financial partners were rattled. iRemedy is a successful company, but a small one—we don't have tens of millions of dollars in cash lying around. And the government does not front the funds for its contracts. We had to rely on private investors and trade financing (at high interest rates). It was a massive amount of cash being sent to China, through intermediaries, before receiving any product.

We were all in; all our chips pushed to the center of the table.

Meanwhile, we thought our London-based intermediary broker was dealing with the factories directly but came to understand that they were working with another intermediary, a Hong Kong import-export firm called Tianjin Materials Company. And we began to suspect that this importer-exporter was screwing both us *and* the factories by demanding lavish cash infusions required by the factories that, despite their claims, never actually made it to the factories at all. Every link on the chain is an opportunity for someone to rip you off.

Deception and embellishment tainted the entire process. The factories' agents were routinely dishonest about how much they were capable of actually producing. This was business as usual even before COVID but the strain of the pandemic, and the extreme sellers' market that had emerged, only encouraged this practice. Generally, it takes a couple months from the time you put in a big order before the manufacturer will complete it. But they were telling us things like, "We'll produce ten million a week in three weeks."

As I mentioned, with medical products, you can't just flip a switch and triple output, and so it goes with needles and syringes. Increasing production to an unprecedented scale is not an overnight process. The factory has to purchase the raw materials, move them to the production site, and tool their machines so they can produce the items with the correct labeling and in accordance with FDA stipulations. We were looking at a time frame of sixty to ninety days.

But at least the gears were turning.

THE WEAKEST LINK

By Land or by Sea

The next question was a thornier one: how do we ship all this inventory to America? Northfield didn't really know. We were in uncharted waters.

We literally sat around with pieces of paper and did some back-of-the-envelope "stupid math"—like how many needles fit in a box, how many boxes in a case, how many cases on a pallet, how many pallets in a container. And then, ultimately, how many containers can we secure on a ship? We called Phil Clayton. He didn't know, nor did our associates at Northfield. When you're dealing with half a *billion* of something, a couple extra cubic inches in a box, multiplied by an untold thousands of boxes, make a big difference in determining how many you can fit on a container or aircraft.

No one even really knew the answer to basic questions like, "How big is a box?" Normally, with just-in-time shipping, you don't have to worry about such details. The product is just *there*, and like clockwork, next week or next month, the next batch will arrive too, just as it always does.

These head-spinning calculations did nothing to alleviate an even bigger problem: ships weren't really shipping. Transoceanic shipping accounts for eighty percent of world trade.[28] It is far and away the primary means of delivering goods around the world. Freighters are to globalization what the subway is to New York City: without it, everything grinds to a halt.

The issue was not so much with the ships as with the containers. Empty containers had piled up in ports in North America and Europe because there were few exports going back the other way, to Asia.[29] We were like, "Where are the containers?" You couldn't just get one. And we were going to need a lot more than one.

Nevertheless, we kept at it, making calls, digitally translating Mandarin into English while pounding coffee, and we managed to lock down empty containers one by one so we'd have some means to transport the needles and syringes as soon as they rolled off the assembly line.

Then, just as we started making headway, the government threw another bureaucratic wrench into our plans: shipping was out of the question—too slow, they said. It takes more than a month to transport goods over the Pacific from China to the west coast.

The DoD again asked us why we couldn't source it domestically, to which we responded that it was impossible. The factories had shut down and moved to China decades ago.

Generally, the DoD is pretty insistent, to put it charitably; when they want something done, they're not diffident about communicating it. They didn't just want us to expedite delivery; they wanted us to guarantee exactly where their stuff was at every moment. How many were made today? Which trucks are they on? Where are the trucks now? When will they reach the warehouse? How many products do you have in XYZ warehouse, in trucks, being loaded? They wanted all that info nonstop, 24/7. We understood their diligence, but it also added to our headache.

If shipping is off the table, there's only one option: air freight. The DoD preferred that because it is much faster and tracking capabilities are better. They were paying for it, and money was no object in the face of a large-scale emergency. But therein lay another conundrum: most air cargo is transported in the belly of passenger jets, and civilian air traffic had also dropped off precipitously. Before March 2020, at any moment from 6 a.m. to midnight, any day of the week, you could look up at the firmament and probably spot at least one jetliner cruising gracefully above the clouds. Now the skies—like the highways, the ports, the factories, the malls, and the schools—had grown quiet.

But like I said, when the DoD wants it done a certain way, you find a way. Anthony and I put our heads together.

"I don't know about you," I said, "but I don't know anything about flying stuff around the world!" iRemedy was an expert at delivery via container ship, but this was a different game. Checking a suitcase at the Delta check-in counter before boarding a flight for vacation was about all I knew about air cargo. I had certainly never delivered a half billion of anything in the belly of a plane.

Fast-forward for a moment to February 27, 2022. If you perused the headlines that day, you might have come across a curious item about the latest casualty in the war in Ukraine: the destruction of the Antonov An-225 Mriya, which was sitting in a hangar in Antonov Airport, the site of a key strategic battle in the early days of the war.

Before it succumbed to shelling, the Antonov was a proud and stately behemoth of the skies: the heaviest plane in the world, boasting the largest wingspan, and since its debut in 1988, used to ferry huge quantities of goods all over the world. (Its final flight was spent airlifting COVID test kits from Tianjin, China, to Denmark).

How big was this thing? Six Blackhawk helicopters could fit in its hold. It was the plane used to transport the International Space Station. The Antonov was a plane that ate other planes for breakfast.

When we learned about the craft during our research, I said, "Yeah, we want that plane!" The largest order of needles and syringes in history warrants one of the largest aircraft ever built.

The Antonov fleet was owned by a company called Volga-Dnepr Airlines, a Russian company. A Texas company was serving as Volga-Dnepr's representative for stateside clients who wanted to charter its planes. In September 2020, the Texas guys came to our office in Florida and brokered a deal between iRemedy and Volga-Dnepr: $600,000 to fly our product from China to Chicago.

Both the Texas company and the Volga guy seemed legitimate, and we were relieved that after months of toil, strife, false starts, setbacks, and shakedowns, finally it seemed like things were coming together. I was thinking, "This is epic! I can't wait to see this thing being unloaded."

Everything was ready to go. All we had to do was book airspace and get an official letter from the State Department to secure traffic rights to land in China. We never expected that in early October 2020, our request to fly the plane would be denied. It seemed cruelly ironic, if not shoot-yourself-in-the-foot counterproductive: the same federal government that was practically begging us to get those needles over here had shot down the best, and seemingly the only, means of doing so. Sure, it was one agency stepping on the toes of another, something that is routine given the vastness of the federal bureaucracy, but it left a bad taste in our mouths.

We fought hard to convince the government to reconsider, but politics had entered the equation. Evidently, Mike Flynn, the retired Army lieutenant general, had received $10,000 in speaking fees from Volga-Dnepr, and the DoD basically blacklisted the company. Volga itself hadn't transgressed, but Flynn's alleged malfeasance tainted everyone around him. It was really just a technicality, and perhaps some politics: other federal agencies, such as FEMA, had chartered Volga-Dnepr, but our contract was with the DoD.

After Volga was blocked, we found ourselves scrambling once again. Basically, we were screwed. And time was running out. We were just a couple months away from the first vaccine rollout. By 2021, almost every man, woman, and child would be clamoring for their jab. That's one or two doses apiece.

And in the last week of September 2020, our problems continued to spiral. Now we had a new adversary: the Chinese Communist Party itself.

CHAPTER 4

THE CHINA SYNDROME

*W*hat's the medical term for clusterf**k?, I wondered, as summer dragged miserably into fall.

Everything that could go wrong did. In the months of red-eyed wrangling and haggling and toiling since the government's order first came in, we had managed to buy up enough raw materials to allow the factories we contracted with to produce the staggering number of five hundred million needles and syringes. This would be the largest single order in the history of the world for this configuration of needles and syringes.

But the factories were way behind schedule and giving us grief. Every day we were assailed with new misdirection, excuses, and false promises—along with demands for even more money. Meanwhile, on the home front, we were struggling to fill our regular orders, our hospital clients were overwhelmed and in a panic like I'd never seen before, and Americans were getting sick, losing their jobs, and dying en masse.

In China, the situation wasn't any better, which probably explains what happened next.

On Sept. 26, 2020, Northfield passed along a message from the chairman of our main factory that the Chinese Communist Party (CCP) would be executing an order to seize 40 percent of the needles we had produced thus far, in order to commandeer them for domestic use rather than export. The chairman expected that this seizure would occur after China's national holidays, set to take place the first week of October. However, said the chairman, a diplomatic visit or communication from the U.S. Embassy in Beijing would potentially preempt the problem, or at least minimize the amount of product that was seized.

We relayed this message to the DoD, which said they would contact the Department of State and figure out next steps. You know that when something is beyond the Department of Defense's purview, you're in trouble!

The Department of State then communicated that the American ambassador was willing to intervene; that he would even personally visit the factory and lean on whoever needed to be leaned on. But when we relayed this message (again, via intermediaries) to the factory chairman, he got cold feet. Now it was apparent to him that Operation Warp Speed was a DoD program, and he thought CCP officials would not take kindly to learning that "their" factory was being utilized in the service of what was he viewed as a U.S. military operation. While the DoD oversees the military, it is a branch of our civilian-controlled government—but in China, the distinction between "civilian government" and the armed forces is inconsequential. To them it was one and the same. Nor would the Party officials appreciate an official visit by the U.S. Ambassador conducted at the behest of the Department of Defense.

So, to avoid antagonizing the CCP further, we had to quietly acquiesce. It was another massive setback, one that drove home the reality of putting your country's medical supply in the hands of a hostile power. Free market capitalism may be as American as apple pie—but it falls apart when the Party wants a big ol' slice of the pie for themselves.

Meanwhile, the biggest question for our role in Operation Warp Speed remained unresolved: how the hell do we get this stuff to American shores?

Fortunately, after the Volga debacle, a new ally emerged: Captain Ryan Croley (Ret.), who worked for Goldbelt. Like Phil Clayton, he was a former military guy. In his mid-forties, sporting a short, clipped haircut, he looks the part. Ryan commanded a Navy SEAL team before retiring from the service, and he brings to his work the calm, cool, ultimate professionalism of a man in that position. But don't mistake his even-keeled demeanor for a lack of fight—he's a badass if there ever was one.

Right away he took control of a sputtering situation and dug into discussions and negotiations with the government about transportation options. Following these talks, the government offered an intriguing alternative: use military transport planes to move the needles and syringes out of China. That would have been a godsend—if those things could deploy troops, tanks, and gear to the battlefields of Afghanistan and Iraq, they could certainly work for us. But the Chinese authorities quickly threw cold water on it: no way were they going to let a military jet bearing the Stars and Stripes land at one of their airports. Besides reasonable national security concerns, the optics for them would have been terrible.

Anthony and I worked closely with Phil and Ryan to find a solution. Phil is very much a color-outside-the-lines, get-it-done-by-any-means-necessary type of guy, a man who brings his martial forcefulness and complete-the-mission ardor to his daily work. His style is different in that respect from Ryan's, but their distinct approaches complemented each other well and they both share a drive to do a good job, whatever the job might be.

Subsequent back-and-forth wheeling and dealing with the federal government turned up another option, in the form of TRANSCOM (United States Transportation Command). TRANSCOM is a "combatant command" under the aegis of the DoD. Among their many operations, they perform airlifts and aviation missions to carry out the functions of the military and the federal government broadly.

Initially I was under the impression that TRANSCOM is akin to a federally owned airline staffed with government employees flying government planes, but they don't really operate like that. TRANSCOM stated that they could get a plane to China and back, but it was complicated: they didn't have their own fleet of aircraft waiting around to be deployed. Instead, they subcontracted another company called Amerijet, which in turn rented a passenger airliner from, of all places, Uzbekistan Airways.

The point person at Amerijet was a man we will call Jimmy, who struck me as arrogant and full of bravado. He didn't exactly inspire confidence. And as it turned out, my instincts were right.

The First Flight: Tianjin Airlift

After so many setbacks and failures and false starts, we were hesitant to get excited about this latest breakthrough. It seemed that Murphy's Law had held true for us since day one. It was hard not to wonder, *What else can go wrong?*

The news around the country was grim. More COVID cases, more deaths. Reports of long-term suffering even among those who had "recovered." Public acrimony over who wears which type of mask in which setting, school lockdowns, and small business closures. No matter where you stood on these issues, it was draining. All Americans were eager to vanquish the virus that was ravaging our way of life. The vaccines that were soon to be rolled out were our best hope, our medical Maginot Line, the last line of defense.

Somehow, these circumstances had brought us to a point where the health of the American public depended on an old 747 belonging to the national airline of a dusty, landlocked Central Asian republic.

Prior to the flight, we were doing calculations about how much product could fit in an aircraft of that size. The seats on the plane had been removed to allow us to stack the thing to the brim. Every cubic inch counted—one extra needle might mean one more person getting protected from the virus. And at a million bucks per flight, you want to be as efficient as possible.

Problems with the impending flight started before the wheels even left the tarmac. Jimmy/Amerijet accused Goldbelt and iRemedy of not having enough available inventory to fill a jet, a complaint he relayed also to the U.S. government. Over the next few days, a series of contentious teleconferences ensued during which Amerijet continued to blame us for not having our shit together, while we stood firm and insisted that we would have the cargo ready and waiting when Amerijet's plane touched down.

"We have inventory waiting at Shanghai Airport. You guys have to pick it up," Ryan shot back.

The mounting problems had tarnished our reputation in the eyes of the DoD, which formally put us and Goldbelt on notice, threatening to cancel the contract because of "nonperformance." And we had already invested around $14 million in deposits in China.

We knew we were right, but there were many unknowns, many plausible scenarios that could result in a half-full plane delivering only a fraction of what we had promised the government. Worse, much of the outcome was out of our control. We'd done everything we could to ensure a successful delivery, but ultimately it would come down to whether the people in China—the factory workers boxing up the product, the truckers spiriting it away to Shanghai, and the logistics personnel at the airport responsible for moving it off the truck and packing it into the plane competently—did what they were supposed to do. Between language barriers, everyone getting COVID, people in isolation or ditching work, the reality was we had no idea what we were going to get. It was a leap of faith. Just wait and see. And hope.

Then, on a calm day in mid-October, the day of the scheduled flight arrived. We watched with bated breath as we tracked it online from Uzbekistan over the arid plains of Central Asia to its destination in China. First leg completed. Then it crisscrossed the hemisphere en route to Chicago O'Hare, where we flew in to be present upon its arrival.

While the plane was still up in the clouds, Goldbelt warned us that their sources informed them the plane had, as feared, taken off mostly empty. The accusations never ceased! We feared that, if true, the government might really cancel our contract. Worst of all, it would be another step backwards in the mission to inoculate America against this terrible disease.

I met Anthony in the cargo terminal of the airport. We were on edge because we had no idea what we would find when that cargo hatch opened. Would it be full? Half-full? Would the needles and syringes be up to code? Did they even pack the correct product? What if the crates were full of fidget spinners and knockoff Nikes?

A full contingent of the military and contracting team met us in a drab airport conference room. Ryan Croley was there too, accompanied by his right-hand woman, Jeantelle "JT" Duhon. I would come to rely upon JT daily, as she proved to be a top-tier operator in the months to come. Then another fellow walked through the door, dressed head-to-toe in Navy khakis, gold buttons and ceremonial medals shining in the fluorescent light. This was Captain Brian Durant. After twenty-eight years of service in the Navy, Durant was on the verge of retirement when he volunteered to help oversee vaccine distribution for Operation Warp Speed—the quintessential "one last mission." Now he was here with us, waiting for a first glimpse at what we all hoped was a successful delivery.

We kept our eyes on the screen until it was confirmed the plane had landed. Phil and I were escorted out to the tarmac to observe its unloading.

Phil is a colorful guy with an unusual hobby: making knives. Picture a burly former soldier pounding superheated metal in his backyard forge. "Listen," said Phil as we walked through the terminal, "if this works out, I'm going to make you a knife."

"Uh, thanks."

Then came the moment of truth as the grounds crew led us to the plane. I think I was literally holding my breath until I was able to actually see with my own eyes that yes, thank God, the fuselage was stacked floor to ceiling, wall to wall, with boxes of needles and syringes. They weren't even on pallets; they were hand-packed individual cases on a "cookie sheet" (a pallet-like ten-by-twenty-foot sheet of metal) to maximize the use of space. The Tianjin logistics crew we had hired did a fine job.

As the crew continued offloading, Ryan and I headed back to the conference room to brief the others. That's when Ryan introduced me to the concept of BLUF: "Bottom Line Up Front," the preferred protocol for briefing military leaders; namely, Durant. In other words, no BS, cut to the chase, don't mince words.

"Don't get into storytelling," said Ryan. "The brass doesn't want stories, background, excuses. They want you to come in and give 'em the bottom line right away. You can't long-talk this guy."

Back in the conference room, I ended up "long-talking" Durant anyway (force of habit!), until Croley shot me a look from across the room. Oops. But it didn't matter. We had done it. The first, we thought, of many such flights to fulfill our commitment to Operation Warp Speed. It was just one battle in a long war, but we had triumphed. I savored that feeling of relief after so many months of disaster.

Why China?

In the rare moments of repose, between harried calls with London, dealing with *Goodfellas*-esque "f—k you, pay me" ultimatums from factory owners in Beijing, and fending off angry missives from DoD functionaries, I had a chance to step back and reflect on the underlying significance of this whole situation. Why were we so dependent on China for getting what we needed?

It shouldn't have been this hard to procure something so integral to the functioning of the healthcare system as needles and syringes. We should have been able to just call up a factory somewhere in America, tell them what we wanted, and have it delivered domestically by rail or truck—or at the very least, by a friendly ally in North America or Europe. How is it that the nation with the largest economy, a proud country that had at one time been the uncontested leader in manufacturing, whose healthcare system (while deeply flawed) is still one of the most sophisticated in the world, had ceded responsibility for making virtually everything you'd find in your local hospital to an authoritarian regime an ocean away?

The answer, of course, is money.

What is casually referred to as "the healthcare industry" is really a patchwork of several distinct industries. It's not a monolith. And profitability is not uniform throughout. Some sectors, like Big Pharma, do pretty well. But healthcare providers? Not so much. Profit margins are thin if not negative.

Providers are perennially saddled with various fixed costs: insurance, technology, construction and maintenance of facilities, doctors' salaries. And they have limited control over how to price their service offerings—insurance companies and Medicaid/Medicare call the shots in that respect.

There's tremendous pressure to minimize costs, but not a lot of wiggle room. So where can you shave off expenses? By trying to get stuff made cheaper elsewhere.

Therefore, in the 1980s, as U.S. healthcare was growing—and becoming astronomically expensive—we in the industry were doing whatever we could to control costs. The United States and Europe had the technology and skilled labor force, counterweighted by high production and labor costs, and high costs for raw materials.

But this was the era when economic globalization was picking up pace and becoming a household word. Markets were breaking open. Capital, labor, and goods were moving at breakneck speed across quickly dissolving borders. So for example, if you're Pfizer and you need to build a billion-dollar plant, suddenly, you don't need to do it in Akron or Stuttgart. You look eastward.

In this way, globalization provided a tantalizing offer. It was the shady guy in the alley who whispers "Psst! Hey!" as he opens his overcoat to show you a line of gleaming, expensive watches purloined from a jewelry store. You know he's up to no good, but damn, $500 bucks for a Rolex? Sure, you'll turn a blind eye to that.

So instead of making stuff at home, companies shifted to a borderless paradigm where "fastest/cheapest/best"—wherever in the world that might be—was the name of the game.

And ever since the eighties and nineties, that place has been China.

An abundance of comparably low-wage, compliant, nonunionized workers was one reason China was attractive to foreign firms. But that wasn't the only factor; indeed, China was not then, and is not now, the country with the lowest labor costs. Rather, as Smil points out, "China provided a combination of other attractors: above all, a centralized one-party government that could guarantee political stability and acceptable investment conditions; a large, highly homogenous and literate population; and an enormous domestic market"—fertile ground for sprouting a "remarkable collusion between the world's largest communist state and a nearly complete lineup of the world's leading capitalist enterprises."[30]

For drug companies, medical device manufacturers, and other players in the healthcare industry, it started with a trickle and grew into a deluge. At the beginning, an occasional product would be made in China. In time, companies shifted more and more of the production for a greater variety of items overseas. Shipping services developed in tandem. Raw materials production increased to supply the factories. The FDA expanded its purview beyond our borders, dispatching inspectors to manufacturing sites abroad to make sure that the products were safe for American consumers. And soon, what began as the import of one-off items coalesced into a thriving industrial ecosystem centered in China. China became the manufacturing center for the U.S. market; the go-to supplier for the world's largest consumer economy and biggest healthcare market.

This process was accelerated by the "just in time" mode of production we discussed in the last chapter. You don't buy a year's worth of groceries and stick it in your garage. You rely on the supermarket to have what you need, when you need it. Hospitals were more than eager to go lean and divest themselves of the burden of maintaining inventory. Healthcare is complicated enough without having that task on their plate as well.

Meanwhile, in the United States, there was little investment in product development or manufacturing, while China was pouring billions of dollars into developing its infrastructure, technology, manufacturing capacity, raw materials access, and billion-strong labor force. It was a big bet that has paid off handsomely. As Yi Wen writes:[31]

> "Thirty-five years ago, China's per capita income was only one-third of that of sub-Sahara Africa. Today, China is the world's largest manufacturing powerhouse: It produces nearly 50 percent of the world's major industrial goods, including crude steel (800 percent of the U.S. level and 50 percent of global supply), cement (60 percent of the world's production), coal (50 percent of the world's production), vehicles (more than 25 percent of global supply) and industrial patent applications (about 150 percent of the U.S. level). China is also the world's largest producer of ships, high-speed trains, robots, tunnels, bridges, highways, chemical fibers, machine tools, computers, cellphones, etc."

Two trends—one in the West, the other in China—met in the middle as they answered each other's needs. The healthcare sector in the U.S. wanted to cut costs and boost profits. The central planners in China wanted to open domestic markets and attract foreign investment.

The result was that an Eastern manufacturing juggernaut emerged with solutions to all the healthcare industry's problems regarding raw material sourcing, production, and delivery. And in this way, the Sino-American medical supply industrial complex was born.

For Americans' part, we accidentally stumbled into this reality. It snuck up on us slowly. The proverbial frog in the pot asking, "Is it hot in here, or is it just me?," unaware that the water is boiling as long as you turn up the temperature bit by bit. *Cuisses de grenouille*, Szechuan-style.

For China, however, as the next chapter will examine, it was all part of a strategy to establish dominance in all areas of manufacturing, including the medical supply business. We were focused on saving money and reducing costs and they were focused on vaulting ahead as the preeminent power on the world stage.

As this medical industrial complex developed, we arrived at a point at which turning back the clock became almost unfathomable. Existing supply lines became entrenched, systematized, and once any system is in place, it requires a great deal of concerted force to dislodge it. In the absence of political will or economic incentive, there was (and is) no pressure on private companies in the U.S. and Europe to alter it. Simply put, China has become very good at everything that a Big Pharma firm or a medical device company needs to make and ship their product. Today, there are certain items, such as specific microchips for ventilators, and certain APIs and drugs, that can only be made in China because they're so sophisticated. No one else has the know-how or the productive capability.

It is technology transfer on a grand scale. China has practiced an aggressive strategy of absorbing—and in some cases outright pilfering—industrial technology from the West, including resorting to industrial espionage and cyber theft.[32] But these cloak-and-dagger methods are dwarfed by a much more mundane process of acquiring foreign technology and processes: Chinese actors simply learn by observing and doing the bidding of Western companies eager to set up shop within China's borders. It was a tradeoff—Chinese firms said, "If you want access to our markets and our manufacturing sector, you have to transfer your IP."

Or, something like the following occurs: say there's a sophisticated machine used in some industrial process that is made in Germany and shipped to a factory in China, where local workers are trained to use it. Eventually they figure out the inner workings of that machine and they just get a cheaper domestic engineer to reproduce it. Now, not only is the German company no longer needed, but Germany doesn't have any workers with the skills to use its own machinery, since they've come to rely on Chinese labor.

State Capitalism

There is another reason for Chinese control of the medical supply: its authoritarian government confers certain economic benefits in managing a quasi-capitalist economy. In short, China is a country run like a corporation.

THE CHINA SYNDROME

As China's economy grew tremendously in the 1990s and early part of the twentieth century, policy wonks and think tanks predicted that economic liberalization would eventually erode the Chinese Communist Party's grip. Capitalism would grease the wheels to democracy, much as it had for the Warsaw Pact nations that emerged from half a century of the Soviet's shadow. Economic liberalization would spur, per conventional wisdom, political liberalization, sapping the power of the communist state.

These predictions were wrong, as Beijing found a way to unite both free market economics and communism in a form of "state capitalism," without ceding its total political control. The sad truth is that the authoritarian approach to managing a mixed economy confers certain competitive advantages.

In the United States, the raison d'etre of a business is, at its most basic level, to make money. Sure, other considerations may inspire owners and shareholders, and hopefully the owners operate with a sense of their place within a society and nation, but the outlook is essentially local. An American factory is not in business to fulfill the aims of the government in Washington. It's trying to make a buck.

In China, it's the opposite: all for-profit industry exists at the behest of, and in service to, the objectives of the Chinese Communist Party and its long-term project to enhance China's status in the world. Business, therefore, operates on a global paradigm: while day to day they're also trying to turn a profit, they are pawns in a bigger, broader game whose rules are dictated from on high.

So while private enterprise and private property do exist, the whole system is still subordinate to the Communist Party and other powerful institutions. The CCP, the State Council, and the military—the entities that run the show at the national level—can reach their fingers down deep locally, anywhere in the mainland, even into a purportedly privately held entity. Property rights are tenuous, and business exists to serve the aims of the state. Theoretically, every company in China can essentially be seized by fiat. Or the CCP or the military can walk into a factory and tell the factory manager, "This is how we're doing things now" or, "You're no longer making washing machines. Now you're making ventilators."

This has been the modus operandi since Deng Xiaoping kicked off China's economic modernization in the eighties. When it came to building its manufacturing sector en route to becoming the world's medical supply closet, China was asking, "How can this mine, this processing plant, this factory, or this logistics company fulfill our national strategic objectives?"

Unsurprisingly, state control over private industry was integral to Beijing's response to COVID, as we experienced ourselves when the CCP seized nearly half of our inventory from our primary factory. As a report from the Congressional Research Service states:

> "In early February 2020, the Chinese government nationalized control of the production and dissemination of medical supplies in China [and] ... transferred authority over the production and distribution of medical supplies from the Ministry of Information Industry and Technology (MIIT) to the NDRC, China's powerful central economic planning ministry. NDRC commandeered medical manufacturing and logistics

down to the factory level and directed the production and distribution of all medical-related production, including U.S. companies' production lines in China, for domestic use."[33]

To be fair, governments in capitalist democracies also intervened in industrial production during the pandemic. For example, the U.S. invoked the Defense Production Act (a law passed in 1950 to bolster the Korean War effort) to compel manufacturers to prioritize COVID-related orders from the federal government, to speed up production of ventilators and respirator masks, to curtail certain exports, to prevent hoarding, and to expedite vaccine production.[34] But these measures are a mere shadow of the vast power the Chinese state has over its thousands of factories, shipping firms, raw materials businesses, and logistics companies.

The most unsettling manifestation of statist control over an ostensibly free market economy is seen in the use of forced labor. There is ample evidence that China impresses incarcerated persons to work in fields and factories without pay, producing hair products, garments, toys, textiles, bricks, and other items.[35] Slavery is the only word for this. Forced labor has been egregiously utilized against the Uyghurs, Muslim ethnic minorities concentrated in the autonomous region of Xinjiang, who have been subject to vicious, systematic repression. Uyghurs have been forced to work in factories in Xinjiang and have also been transported to toil in plants in other regions of China, "broadening the risk of forced labor in supply chains" that produce goods used by you and me.[36]

We inadvertently brushed against the wretched practice of slave labor in our own work. When the Biden administration launched a free COVID test kit program in early 2022, those half-billion test kits had to come from somewhere. iRemedy was involved in the procurement, and naturally, we turned to China, since the U.S. couldn't make nearly that many on its own. One of the test kit manufacturers we were dealing with hired ten thousand laborers within a week. How was that even possible? We heard rumors from our business contacts that many (or most) of those newly "hired" individuals were, in essence, slaves, as well as children. As we probed further, we traced that firm back up through several parent companies and found that at the top was a military-owned company that had been banned from bidding on federal contracts because of its use of slave labor. Needless to say, we cut ties with that company immediately, though the practice, unfortunately, persists. But how do you compete financially with a competitor using slave labor?

In many respects, China is not simply a country run like a company; it's a company run like a prison.

The Second Flight: Too Good to Be True

After the first successful flight with TRANSCOM, Ryan took the reins from Phil and handled managing the government, a role he performed with aplomb. He satisfied the DoD's demands for information by keeping them abreast of which factories were developing which needles on which days, and where those needles were presently—whether on the shipping bay of the factory, on trucks crossing China, staged at an export location, on airplanes, or being offloaded in Chicago. Basically, if we produced a needle, the government would know about it.

Ryan's adroitness with handling government affairs freed Anthony and me up to focus more on operations and ensure everything was on schedule with the factories in China. There was nothing we could do about the CCP taking our product—beyond blind hope that it wouldn't happen again— but we managed to pivot and sign on four additional smaller factories to make up for the loss. As for any kind of financial compensation for what was basically theft of our merchandise, forget it. No one in China gave a damn, and the U.S. government was only concerned with getting what they had ordered. We simply had to eat the cost.

Next, we made arrangements with TRANSCOM for a second flight. It was the same deal: TRANSCOM chartered Amerijet, which chartered a plane from Uzbekistan.

Arranging the flight was only one of the myriad challenges in securing the delivery. There are many moving parts to think about. How many trucks are leaving the factories with how many boxes of needles? How many will pass Chinese customs and how long will that take? How long will it take to load them all onto the plane?

You have to coordinate output of factories, overland transport to the shipping point at the airport, jets flying in to pick up that material—and all of this is arranged through intermediaries twelve hours ahead who don't speak English.

Nevertheless, we were on top of it.

But then we hit a major snag.

The plane was due to land in Shanghai at 2 p.m. local time. A few days before the flight, we got a call from the logistics company working at the airport; we dealt with a Chinese gentleman there I know only as James. (Many Chinese people adopt Western names when working or associating with non-Chinese speakers.)

"Your jet is arriving at 2 and leaving at 3. We can't load it in one hour," he said.

And he was absolutely right. It's not just loading the cargo; you have to factor in customs, inspection, paperwork—and customs was already short-staffed because of COVID.

One hour to clear customs *and* fill a 747 with medical gear? It was just impossible.

Furious, we asked TRANSCOM for an explanation. They didn't really respond. Then we pressed Uzbekistani Airlines for answers, to no avail. "We don't care, we'll fly it out empty if we have to. In fact, we prefer it—we don't burn as much fuel," they said. They were getting paid either way, so they didn't give a damn about whether the cargo went on the plane or not.

I was flabbergasted. This wasn't just incompetence; it was fraud!

James was also outraged. But he was just one logistics manager in an airport and in no position to pull strings.

We reported it up the chain of command; some back-and-forth ensued but we received no real answers. The day of the flight arrived, with no solution. We just had to hope for a miracle.

That morning, I woke up at an ungodly hour (as I often did those days) to check messages that our overseas contacts had sent during my fitful night's sleep. Paula, our coordinating resource in London, had sent me a message on WhatsApp that started with "Tony, I have no words." She went on to explain that the jet indeed had turned around and left, empty. Our teams in

Shanghai and London were in shock. Presently, it was in the air, Chicago-bound, with not a single needle in its hold.

I was furious. I knew Captain Durant would be furious. The DoD was going to rage, not only at the fact that a million dollars of taxpayer funds had been squandered, but more importantly, that several million fewer needles would be added to a vaccination arsenal where they were desperately needed.

Wide awake, I called Anthony and together, we commiserated as we pulled up the flight tracking website and watched our plane arc across the digital sky—a little faster than normal, it seemed, now that its cargo hold was empty.

It was going to be a long day.

Ryan has a rule that has served him well in his military and government work: "Bad news doesn't get better with time." When something goes wrong, don't sit on it or try to do damage control before divulging it; report it immediately. Conveying bad news effectively is part of his job. So he went to our DoD contacts and informed them what happened. Their reaction was pretty much what I expected—they were apoplectic. The government immediately launched an investigation.

We demanded a response from TRANSCOM/Uzbekistani Airlines, which merely tried to shift blame. They accused us of not having our cargo ready to be loaded, claiming we had failed to clear customs, leaving the pilots and crew with no choice but to take off without the cargo. It was a blatant lie, and they knew it, but it was their word against ours.

The empty flight was the worst thing that could have happened. It marred our reputation and made us look incompetent, or worse—just another deceitful outfit trying to profit from the pandemic and exploit the government's largesse.

We pleaded our case to government officials—that it was the fault of Uzbekistani Airlines, which had refused to change the flight plan to allow time for loading—but it sounded like buck-passing to them. After all, *we* were the ones that had been awarded the contract.

We put together our own little investigation and through our contacts in Shanghai Airport, we were able to obtain CCTV footage of the staging area where our millions of needles and syringes were neatly stacked, signed, sealed, and delivered, ready for onloading. That was proof positive that the fault was somewhere between Amerijet and the Uzbek pilots.

That helped restore our reputation, but again, the loss of money wasn't the government's chief concern. That was just business. They wanted the needles. "Where are they and how many will be here tomorrow?" they demanded to know.

All this drama, all these cross-border hurdles, all this wrangling to secure the medical supply, is what the average American does not see when they drop their prescription off at the pharmacy, or when the seasonal flu shot goes into their arm, or when their doctor snaps on a pair of nitrile gloves and says, "Let me have a look." In good times and bad, pandemic or not, the fact remains that we are locked into dependence on China for our healthcare the way a gambling addict is in deep with his bookie.

Globalizing the supply chain worked well for a while, but when COVID struck, the system that we had all been lulled into embracing for its convenience, efficiency, and profitability was suddenly a menace—why "just in time" turned into having to fight hard just to get a single plane to reach us.

Healthcare organizations are preoccupied with an immediate, local problem: they are taking care of patients, physicians, staff. They're optimizing to meet the needs of their community's healthcare demands. It's not their mandate to think about national security risks. But each day that passes, the time bomb of the medical supply ticks closer and closer to the next big detonation.

Bad for us; good for China. The next chapter will look at this problem in the context of China's decades-long project for global hegemony, and what that might mean for America's future.

CHAPTER 5

THE DRAGON'S PLAN FOR WORLD DOMINATION

I was just a teenager when President Nixon's plane landed in Shanghai on a frigid February day in 1972. This momentous occasion marked the re-establishment of diplomatic relations with the People's Republic of China, where no U.S. president had ever set foot. At the time, the world's most populous state was basically a peasant nation, broke and irrelevant, with a standard of living vastly inferior to our own.

Yet in the decades since Nixon shook hands with Mao, America's power and prestige has been on a slow decline, while China's has been ascendent. Today, China threatens to displace the U.S. as the world's superpower, jeopardizing our number-one spot in the global arena and perhaps the comfortable way of life Americans see as their birthright.

I'm not a political scientist, a China scholar, or a national security expert, and I do not claim to be an authority on these affairs. But my depth of experience doing business in and with China has allowed me to understand better than most how much of our prestige and competitive advantage has been ceded to our rival across the Pacific. The medical supply chain is the tip of the iceberg—just one plank in a multifaceted project to rule the world. And if that sounds hyperbolic, don't take my word for it: look at the evidence yourself. It's all out there in the open.

I'm writing this book to sound the alarm, because while the China threat receives periodic soundbite lip service among congresspeople, the White House (regardless of who currently sits in the Oval Office), and the media, no one is really taking action to counter the danger.

Put simply, Beijing is outmaneuvering Washington economically, militarily, technologically, diplomatically, and industrially. We cannot understand the risk that foreign dependence on medical supplies poses to our healthcare system without first viewing it in the context of a larger and even more perilous geopolitical contest between two superpowers—one on the rise, the other struggling to patch up the cracks.

The Hundred-Year Marathon

One of the best works of scholarship on the subject is Michael Pillsbury's *The Hundred-Year Marathon: China's Secret Strategy to Replace America as the Global Superpower.* Pillsbury, a veteran of the U.S. national security apparatus and a fluent Mandarin speaker, describes how in the mid-twentieth century, Chinese hawks who had the ear of Mao Zedong embarked on a long-term plan "to avenge a century of humiliation and aspired to replace the United States as the economic, military, and political leader of the world by the year 2049 (the one hundredth anniversary of the Communist Revolution)."[37]

The titular word "secret" in the title, while intriguing, is something of a misnomer: this project is hiding in plain sight, but Western experts on China, including the national security establishment in the U.S., have turned a blind eye to Beijing's aggressive turn. While Pillsbury draws on intelligence assets and unpublished materials, much of the supporting evidence in his book comes from published Party and government documents which, while open-source, are illegible to Western experts who, even if they speak Mandarin, wouldn't understand the CCP's unique brand of doublespeak. Encoded in that language of deceit are the blueprints for a plan to unseat the U.S. and seize the throne.

Deception, concealment (of one's motives), and patience, rather than overt displays of force, are the preferred tactics for the hundred-year marathon, says Pillsbury. "The lesson is famous in China: 'Never ask the weight of the emperor's cauldrons.' In other words, don't let the enemy know you're a rival, until it is too late for him to stop you. On the international level, if you are a rising power, you must manipulate the perceptions of the dominant world power to not be destroyed by it."[38]

The hundred-year marathon is based on a patient cultivation of economic, military, and diplomatic power until the right conditions are in place. In Chinese military doctrine, there is a traditional concept called *shi*, a difficult-to-translate word that refers to a quasi-mystical "alignment of forces or propensity of things to happen which only a skilled strategist can exploit to ensure victory over a superior force"—vaguely akin to "the Force" in the Star Wars universe. Shi consists of "deceiving others into doing your bidding for you, and waiting for the point of maximum opportunity to strike" (p. 44).

So far, Beijing has deployed these tactics masterfully, since, Pillsbury argues convincingly, the U.S. and its allies have not only failed to put forth a coherent plan to check Chinese hegemony, we have willingly encouraged it! Pillsbury points to several "false assumptions" the United States maintains toward China that encourages Chinese hegemony right under our nose. Specifically, these include the notion that engagement necessarily leads to cooperation; that China is on the road to democracy; the idea of China as a "fragile flower"; the notion that China wants to be like us (they do not); and that Chinese hawks are weak.

Americans have bought into the narrative of Chinese moderacy—that the hawks are marginal players. Similarly, the national security establishment, according to Pillsbury, misinterprets periodic flashes of China's power as anomalies and not part of a strategic pattern; or they miss the many signs that China is ratcheting up its aggressiveness—as the balance of *shi* grows ever more favorable—for a decisive move to displace the United States once and for all.[39]

And as I've discussed extensively in the preceding chapters, the West has happily, and perhaps greedily, facilitated this rise. We've exported our manufacturing (and with it, many of our citizens' middle-class jobs). We've freely given, or carelessly made available for theft and copying, our intellectual property. This blind-eye blitheness is the same kind of ho-hum, everything-is-fine attitude that got us into the medical supply mess during COVID. We were too myopic, too lulled into a false sense of security that the system would bend but not break.

Now China has us by the qiú, and it doesn't seem to want to let go.

Economy

What defines America's superpower status, even more than its diplomatic heft or its military might, is its indomitable economy. The conventional benchmark for the size of a nation-state's economy is gross domestic product. A lot of stock is put into GDP as a measure of overall economic strength. Presently, China's GDP lags behind the U.S. by about $6 trillion,[40] but it is likely to pull ahead sometime in the 2030s.[41]

By other metrics, China has already surpassed us economically. For example, in "share of economic power" (a statistic that combines share of world trade, global GDP, purchasing power parities, and net capital exports), China is out in front.[42] In 2020, 124 of the firms on the Fortune 500 list were Chinese, compared with 121 in the United States.[43] Since 1990, China has enjoyed white-hot economic growth rates (averaging double digits, even as the rate has slowed in recent years), while the U.S. growth rate has hovered around 3 percent during the same period.[44,45]

China has long been a manufacturing/production powerhouse, but as its wealth continues to grow, it is also becoming a consumer juggernaut, attracting prestigious global firms that want to sell to its burgeoning middle and upper class. Given its population of 1.4 billion people, it's hard for the U.S. to keep pace without a forward-thinking economic plan, which Washington has sorely neglected.

Technology and Infrastructure

Any capable business leader knows that once your business starts turning a profit, you don't run out and spend the money on yourself; you redirect the surplus back into the business so that its growth compounds. And China, Inc. has shrewdly channeled the wealth generated by its strong economy back into developing its technology and infrastructure.

In its stated quest to be *the* preeminent leader in science and innovation by 2050 (right around the projected terminus of the hundred-year marathon[46]), Beijing has poured billions into its research and development budget for science and technology—second-most in the world, and far surpassing the U.S.[47] China is also advancing rapidly in the strategically critical technologies of the future, including green energy, nuclear power, AI, advanced computing, and robotics. It's also leading the rollout of 5G networks.[48]

Meanwhile, according to a 2020 report by the Congressional Research Service, "China is also seeking to make gains in strategic sectors—such as telecommunications, microelectronics, and semiconductors—in which the government undertook extraordinary measures to sustain research and development and manufacturing during the COVID-19 outbreak in China."[49]

Likewise, the Chinese are running circles around us when it comes to infrastructure. The Chinese government has built myriad new railways, airports, bridges, dams, power plants (including solar and wind), and highways that boost the economy and contribute to a better quality of life generally. Ongoing one *trillion*-dollar infrastructure initiatives will yield sources of renewable energy (wind and solar power bases), the world's longest water tunnel, greener urban spaces, high speed rail, and new data centers.[50]

Americans, meanwhile, look glumly at their deteriorating roads, collapsing bridges, and lead-poisoned water systems (as in my hometown of Flint, Michigan)—infrastructural decay that inhibits economic growth and jeopardizes public health. Much of our infrastructure was built decades ago, and shows its age. A 2021 Council on Foreign Relations report stated that "U.S. infrastructure is both dangerously overstretched and lagging behind that of its economic competitors, particularly China."[51]

Our democratic system used to excel at planning, financing, and building major public works projects. Now, many capital projects perish in a "death by a thousand committees," thanks to bickering between jurisdictions or private-public entities, or simply failing to garner the political will (and funding) necessary.

China's infrastructure boom is largely a function of its authoritarian government: it is capable of leveraging huge amounts of capital and manpower on centrally planned public works projects, with scant regard for norms of public safety or worker protection. Obviously, we shouldn't mimic that system. But we must find a way to demonstrate that our federalist, republican government is capable of keeping pace and building big, useful things.

Military

Cavalcades of menacing missiles, tanks, and troops rolling through downtown Moscow remains an iconic and enduring historical memory of the Soviet Union—a big show intended to stir patriotic feelings in its citizens as much as put its capitalist adversaries on notice.

China stages annual military parades too, but conspicuous militarization to intimidate enemies with bold displays of strength is not a key feature of Beijing's military strategy. On the contrary, China mostly seeks to downplay its military expansion even as it becomes regionally more aggressive—a delicate balancing act.

As Pillsbury writes:

"[The hawks] think China instead needs a force level large enough to support economic growth but small enough to avoid prematurely provoking the American hegemon. However … China could decide to cast aside its self-imposed constraints on military spending in the final phases of a multidecade competition—once it's too late for America to stop them. Chinese writings on the revolution in military affairs have hinted for two decades about the ideal time to break out, which is still many years ahead."[52]

Statistics give us some insight into the state of China's military project. In terms of the number of battle-ready ships and submarines, China has us beat.[53] Its number of active frontline military personnel (2.3 million) exceeds ours.[54] President Xi Jinping is encouraging an arms buildup to boost its nuclear arsenal, modernize its aircraft carriers, develop hypersonic missiles, and invest in AI and cyberwarfare research.[55] Xi has set 2035 as the deadline for this modernization, with an eye toward having a "world-class force" capable of fighting and winning any armed conflict by 2049.[56]

The United States still possesses the most powerful military in the world, but China doesn't necessarily need more firepower and manpower to gain the upper hand. Chinese hawks like to refer to the Assassin's Mace, a weapon well-known in Chinese folklore, like the slingshot David used to fell Goliath.[57] The idea is that asymmetric warfare allows a smaller opponent to defeat a larger one. Cyber warfare, jamming enemy communications, directed-energy weapons, electromagnetic pulse weapons, smart bombs, antiradar systems, electronic warfare, antisatellite weapons, and antiship ballistic missiles (dubbed "aircraft carrier killers") are examples of such asymmetric weapons that China is investing in.[58]

Recent events might contradict Pillsbury's assertion that the moment for "breaking out" is still decades away. Unabashed shows of force in the South China Sea and around Taiwan—the biggest flashpoint of American and Chinese jockeying—suggest a kind of muscle-flexing that may signal an impending graduation from the "lay low" phase to the "we're challenging you head-on" phase. As an example, consider Beijing's belligerent response to Nancy Pelosi's 2022 visit to the island, when China conducted bellicose air, sea, and missile maneuvers around the island. And China's heavy-handed rule of semi-autonomous Hong Kong, especially evident in the violent suppression of the 2019-2020 democracy protests there, could serve as a model of future Chinese rule in Taiwan.

China claims Taiwan as its own, and the U.S. insists it will defend the island in the face of a Chinese incursion. Whether and how China will attempt to take Taiwan by force, and what an American response would look like, is anyone's guess. But it's a dangerous game of chicken.

Japan has also been a target of Chinese antagonism in recent years. A state-sponsored "anti-Japan demonization program" to whip up nationalist fervor not just among its own citizens but among other Asian populations, including Japan's own domestic audiences, is evidence of this anti-Japanese hostility.[59] This is partly due to historical grievances and territorial disputes with Tokyo, but also because Japan, as America's closest Asian ally, serves as a kind of proxy for our own global presence. It's a challenge: if the U.S. can't come to the defense of its friends, then its status as a world leader is weakened.

Diplomacy

Superpower status requires more than a booming economy and an indomitable military. It means exercising international statecraft to curry favor, cultivate influence, sideline one's competitors, and command respect and influence as a leader on the world stage.

Since the last bombs fell in the Second World War, the U.S. has painstakingly cultivated a network of foreign alliances that has benefited us tremendously and engendered a global order that is also favorable to our allies. For example: NATO, our close economic and diplomatic partnerships with Europe, and our friendly relations with the important states of Japan and Korea. These relationships maintain peace and security by preventing armed conflict and facilitating global trade in a way that is economically beneficial to all.

In short, even a superpower can't go at it alone. Maintaining networks of political allies and trade partners with common interests within a shared sphere of influence is essential to a long-term hegemonic project.

No wonder, then, that China is also asserting itself in the international arena, putting forth its own vision of a global order in which Beijing, not Washington, leads the way. Xi Jingping has sought a more prominent, more active role in international summits, which plays well for optics-friendly snapshots in the papers, but also has a real-world, *realpolitik* impact, in that it reinforces the message that he, not the current leader of the U.S. or France or Germany, is the one to talk to whenever heads of state gather.

China is not exactly trying to set up a rival network of authoritarian regimes to counter the Pax Americana, like the Allies against the Axis in WWII; there is no "anti-NATO" afoot. But Beijing does have a much more relaxed stance toward America's geopolitical adversaries, such as North Korea (its only formal ally)[60] and Russia. China has been muted in its opposition to Russia's war in Ukraine, in part because Russia is a check on American power and in part because a Russian triumph in its war of aggression against its neighbor improves the prospects of China achieving the same with Taiwan, while severely discrediting the NATO-US-EU bloc that is aiding Ukraine in its fight.[61] The "Global Security Initiative" which seeks to undermine the U.S. defense alliance with Korea, Japan, Europe, and others is another of Xi's initiatives.[62]

Meanwhile, China is leveraging soft power to lure smaller states out of the West's orbit. State-funded programs that promote Chinese language and culture abroad, international aid in the forms of grants and loans, and financing capital works projects, such as the Belt and Road Initiative, have been launched to brighten Beijing's image abroad and deliver material benefits in those countries.[63]

China's frenzied domestic infrastructure program has expanded beyond its own territory as it funds the construction of major projects in foreign states.[64] Railroads, airports, skyscrapers, dams, and seaports have been built to facilitate trade with China and bring beneficiaries of these projects within Beijing's sphere of influence.

And it's not just the developing world where China is building foundations (literally). China has been building in the busy Greek port of Piraeus, and Chinese firms have made heavy investments in other ports around Europe.

Students of international relations describe the "Kindleberger trap" (named for economist Charles Kindleberger), which posits that countries that seek to become world leaders must provide global public goods (security guarantees, access to lucrative markets, maintenance of free trade, a healthy environment, etc.)—in other words, if you want to make friends, you've gotta give something in return. This is a stumbling block for China, which is less transparent, less generous, and less invested in maintaining the existing security order than the United States.[65] "In many developing countries, construction with Chinese finance has yielded some much-needed infrastructure. But a number of "white elephants" and the debts piling up have dealt a serious blow to China's image as a competent and reliable partner of the Global South," writes Plamen Tonchev in *The Diplomat*.[66] The Belt and Road Initiative may mitigate that. Only time will tell.

China's Challenges

To be fair, it would be inaccurate to portray China as an unstoppable behemoth. The threat it poses is stark, but the country is hardly untroubled. Cracks have formed on the surface of its vaunted economy. As of this writing, exports have declined, the real estate market has tanked (affecting other sectors), and domestic demand is weak.[67] Household debt has spiked,[68] and China's population actually *fell* in 2022, for the first time in sixty years—a harbinger of deeper trouble to come.[69]

America's Decline, China's Rise?

As I've mentioned, I grew up in Flint, Michigan, in a General Motors family. My dad was an executive with GM during the heyday of the American automotive industry. For my first business, which I started in 1980, I ran a direct mail service, and my biggest clients were the UAW locals, which hired me to mail out union newspapers.

At that point, globalization had only just begun the process of radically envisioning the U.S. and world economies. Things were still good, but the highwater mark for American industry had passed. What happened next is a well-known tale. Cheap labor, raw materials access, lack of worker and environmental protections, and other factors led to a hemorrhaging of American manufacturing jobs, once a reliable path to the middle class, as the factories moved east, particularly to China.

The auto industry was hit especially hard. I saw the damage to the community as a result. Flint, epitome of this Rust Belt rot, never recovered. Today, Flint is most often associated with the water crisis of 2014-2017, where lead from corroding water pipes poisoned thousands, including many children. At the same time that China is building vast infrastructure projects at home and abroad with dizzying speed, the U.S. struggles even to supply a midsized city with safe drinking water.

The hollowing out of my hometown, and so many others like it, has left an impression on me. Now, I understand it as part of a bigger and more insidious picture. While most Americans view deindustrialization as circumstantial, or even accidental—various economic actors responding rationally, if selfishly, to changing economic conditions—in China, it was no accident. Turning China into the world's manufacturing hub, for medical supplies and basically everything else, has been a central plank in a long-term, multifaceted project for global hegemony.

Our loss was their gain. However, I am not arguing that all geopolitics is a no-holds-barred, winner-take-all, zero-sum conquest. On the contrary, everyone benefits when states, even nominal competitors, co-exist in a cooperative arena based on mutual interests. The rivalry between Washington and Beijing is not a Manichean struggle. And we must acknowledge that Washington's desire to maintain superpower status is motivated chiefly by self-interest—just as with any state, really. Nor am I asserting that the proper response to Chinese aggression is to launch our own brand of anti-Chinese jingoism.

I am, however, saying that we—by which I mean all of us, public officials, the national security apparatus, the business community, and the American populace—must recognize what is actually happening in Beijing. That China is biding its time as it gathers its forces, in a campaign that is each day becoming less "hiding in plain sight" and more provocatively visible. Americans remain blissfully ignorant of China's project, allowing China to move ahead unfettered. As Pillsbury says, it's easy to win a race when you're the only one who knows it's begun.[70]

It's weird for Americans to face these issues after eighty years of holding superpower status. It makes us complacent, if not arrogant. We've never had another country tell us the way things are going to go, so we can hardly fathom it. Let's not let our American exceptionalism blind us to the realities afoot. Instead, let's do what we've been good at as a nation, what let us become leaders in the first place: face our problems head on, roll up our sleeves, and fix it. In Chapter 10, I'll talk about solutions, with a focus on resolving the medical supply issue that is the subject of this book, but also how the U.S. can check an ascendant China before it's too late.

CHAPTER 6

INDIA'S PHARMA DEFENSE PLAN

In the midst of the needle scramble, Anthony embarked on another mission: helping the government of a midsized Latin American country source the vaccine. Their efforts had been foiled by the same supply and demand problems as the needles: everyone wanted it, there wasn't yet enough to go around, and the few places lucky enough to have surplus production were on the other side of the world. They couldn't get it anywhere, so they turned to us.

Anthony was determined to find a supplier, so it was back on the merry-go-round of 24/7 calls, emails, and WhatsApp conversations with health officials, factory owners, and various middlemen, until he made contact with Ágnes Bognár, managing director of a Budapest-based firm which specializes in the procurement and wholesale of medicines, medical devices, cosmetics, and nutritional products. That company procures drugs for the whole European market. Almost all the pharmaceuticals used in Europe come from factories in India. Despite China's massive industry, India actually produces *more* finished drugs than China (though most active pharmaceutical ingredients—APIs— are still Chinese in origin). For this reason, India has been dubbed the world's medicine cabinet.

But when you open up the bathroom mirror to look at what's actually *in* the world's medicine cabinet, it's a little like Alice crossing through the looking glass—you're about to enter an upside-down terrain where few things make sense, nothing is as it seems, and getting what you want means negotiating with a lot of Mad Hatter and Cheshire Cat types—if the Mad Hatter owns a pharma plant, and the Cheshire Cat works for the Ministry of Health.

India: China's Number-One Competitor

India's rise as a pharma manufacturing center began in the 1970s but really took off in the last couple decades, mostly in response to market pressures: they saw their neighbor to the north raking it in from Western drug companies that had set up shop in China, so Indian firms wanted in on the game. Foreign companies were only too happy to oblige. Like China, India has a vast labor pool (1.39 billion people live on the subcontinent), low production costs, and lax environmental safeguards (chemistry can be a dirty business)—all of which made it an appealing locale for drug production.

Today, production of surgical tools, medical devices, and protective gear are still concentrated in China, and that is unlikely to change. But India leads the way in generic drug production. Of 342 factories worldwide that make more than ten active ingredients for the U.S. market, 183 are located in India.[71]

What do I mean by generics? In the world of pharma, you've got generics and brand names. When a drug company's patent on a drug expires, other manufacturers are free to produce it (just under a name that's different from the brand name). It's a *vast* market that matters much more than the name-brand market. Ninety percent of the prescription drugs Americans take are generics.[72] Europeans and Africans—whose main supplier is India too—also depend on generics much more than their name brand counterparts.

India's status as the generics kingpin conceals one important fact: China still controls the raw materials and APIs with which drugs are made. Seventy percent of bulk drugs used in Indian pharma production come from its neighbor to the north,[73] and upwards of 90 percent for certain drugs.[74] So even if Indian factories were pumping out a billion pills a minute, if the material origin of those pills is under Beijing's thumb, then India remains a subordinate player in its own game.

Not only is this bad for business (because Indian companies pay a pretty penny for those imported APIs, versus making them domestically), but it is a huge vulnerability, for the same reasons we've talked about already. China could pull the plug at any time, for any reason. Relations between China and India are tepid, at best, and India recognizes that a trade war, pandemic-related lockdown, or armed conflict (a distinct possibility: in the last couple decades the two powers have come to blows over disputed border areas) could precipitate an overnight shutdown of the API pipeline.

India got a bitter taste of this during COVID: when the Chinese drug industry slowed down, so did India's. Supply chains were disrupted, API prices soared, and the assembly lines ground to a halt. A hard pill to swallow, indeed. And as I've said before, if it happened once, it can, and probably will, happen again.

In response, India is betting big on developing its production of raw materials to supply its busy pharmaceutical plants. The most eye-popping example of this strategy so far is the construction of a massive "pharma city" in Hyderabad, the unofficial capital of the country's generics industry (what Hubei province is to China). The size of fourteen thousand soccer fields, Hyderabad Pharma City is expected to employ *half a million* people working for over a hundred drug companies churning out penicillin, antimalarials, diabetes drugs, and all kinds of vital products Grandma and Grandpa—and you—will be popping at the breakfast table.[75]

India recognizes that importing most of the active ingredients from China not only jeopardizes the health of a vital industry, it's a national security risk. Rosemary Gibson writes in *China Rx: Exposing the Risks of America's Dependence on China for Medicine,* "Unlike the mainstream media in the United States, the Indian press doesn't hesitate to report the health and national security risks of dependence on China. A *Financial Express* headline blared, 'Indian Bulk Drug Industry Faces Chinese Threat,' because of its dependence on China ("bulk drugs" are another term for APIs). The *Economic Times* published a story about the risks to national security, and the opening line was, 'Imagine a situation where a soldier's medical kit is running out of essential drugs on a battle front.' A deterioration in India's relationship with China could trigger China to withhold supplies of vital components in essential medicines."[76]

Time will tell if India is actually able to wean itself off dependence on China, but it raises a question: if India recognizes the threat of China and is taking steps to remedy it, why aren't we?

Anthony in Pharmaceutical Wonderland

Anthony was running into a lot of hitches.

He flew out to Budapest to meet with Agnes Bey face to face, transiting through desolate airports, normally Europe's busiest, that were now eerily calm, devoid of tourists and full of shuttered shops and darkened hallways.

Agnes and her firm were legit; real professionals and experts in the byzantine world of the Indian generics industry. They had a permanent staff member in India, so crucial was that country to the company's operations and, by extension, the European drug market.

One might think India does business like the West, but Anthony quickly learned that's not the case. There is a mind-boggling amount of red tape. You have to grease the wheels by getting various dubious officials to approve your production; then you must obtain another set of permits, from different government agencies, for export. To put it bluntly, it requires a lot of bribes, bureaucracy, and bull.

Agnes had an ongoing contract with Dr. Reddy's, which was manufacturing one of the COVID vaccines. Dr. Reddy's is big, the Coca-Cola of Indian generics, with a $8.8 billion market cap.[77] (They're also planning on setting up shop at the Hyderabad Pharma City.) We hoped we could cut in on that. But to get access to Dr. Reddy's factories, you need various permits from four to five different parties (all of whom represent different government agencies and jurisdictions). You need approvals from the Minister of Health and an export permit from the Drug Controller General of India, part of the Directorate General of Health Services.

You need the green light from local "officials" too, such as the governor of the state where the factory is located. India has twenty-eight different states and eight "union territories." It was not unlike China, where working with a factory might entail negotiating with a local Communist Party official who is like a de facto co-CEO of that factory.

First we would need to obtain approval from the local state government to begin the manufacturing process. In order to do this, we would have to prove that we had a verified foreign government committing to purchase. Then we would have to get approval for the timeline of production. Once production was done, we would need approval to move the product, under strict conditions (cold-chain storage, batch number tracing, etc.) to the port of export. Then from there the export approval process would begin.[78]

As Anthony struggled to keep things moving, he found that the criteria for securing the necessary permits were wildly subjective, and seemingly arbitrary. There was too much "discretionary approval" driving the process. Whether you were accepted or denied seemed up to some random functionary's mood at the moment he got your email. And multiple government officials were asking for money up front to "secure the rights to start manufacturing." It might not have technically been a bribe, but it certainly felt like one. You had to buy your place in line.

India also demanded a mountain of paperwork from our client country, which both added to the mess of red tape and offended representatives of that government, who felt they were being dismissed as an illegitimate buyer. In addition to jumping through a thousand hoops in Pharma-Wonderland, Anthony had to mediate between two governments representing two radically different cultures. It turned into a battle of egos, but India wouldn't budge. Getting these two parties in accord was an insurmountable burden on top of everything else, and ultimately, we just couldn't get the deal done.

Now, to be fair, maybe the pandemic had exaggerated the rigors and requirements of this process of drug procurement. The circumstances were unusual, and everyone—every government, every hospital, every health organization—was trying to lock down an expensive and complex drug that was still scarce. But it does highlight some of the problems of doing business in India. And that's just the tip of the iceberg.

Why India Is Not a Better Alternative than China

Perhaps you are thinking, "India is a capitalist democracy. It's friendlier toward the U.S. Doesn't that make it a better alternative to China?" The answer is slightly, perhaps, but not much. And in some ways India is worse.

There are three drawbacks to hitching our nation's medical supply (drug supply in particular) star to India's wagon: 1) poor quality control; 2) geopolitics; and 3) simple geography.

First, Indian factories have well-documented quality control problems. Even China, for all its issues, is pretty good when it comes to ensuring that its medical products are safe, compliant, and up to code. It's an authoritarian country, and if there's one thing authoritarian countries are good at, it's enforcing regulations. How many countries can keep a billion people locked in their apartments, as China did during COVID?

Things are a little more lax in India, where power is much less centralized and enforcement is not conducted with the same diligence, creating more opportunities for rule-bending. Corruption and corner-cutting is part of doing business. In addition, you have to deal with the complications of India's cultural geography: more than a billion people who speak at least twenty-two languages (those are just the official ones!) spread across thirty-six states and territories. "The sheer size and fragmented nature of the Indian market can also present a challenge for investors and businesses. Indian states are often compared to individual nations, given their size and diversity in language, culture, talent and infrastructure. This creates a considerable variance in business landscapes," notes a report by Wolters Kluwer, a Dutch information services company.[79]

In China, pretty much everyone speaks Mandarin, and the government is essentially a monolithic, top-down organ. In India it is a patchwork of various crisscrossing jurisdictions and localities, and the factory owner in one state might not even speak the same language (literally) as the health minister in the next.

This environment is conducive to quality control shortcomings. Technically, any factory making drugs for export to the States must be FDA-approved. But many Indian factories do *not* have FDA certification. And even approved factories are not inspected by the FDA with the same rigor that they would be if they were in U.S. territory. (We'll talk more about the role of the FDA abroad in Chapter 8).

As I said before, if you're manufacturing minifridges and you cut some corners, the worst that can happen is your beer gets warm or your milk spoils. If you are making drugs, the consequences can be downright tragic. That is exactly what happened recently in Gambia, where twenty-two children died as a result of ingesting tainted cough syrup produced by Maiden Pharmaceuticals, based in Delhi.[80] The World Health Organization quickly issued a warning that the contaminated product can cause "abdominal pain, vomiting, diarrhea, inability to pass urine, headache, altered mental state, and acute kidney injury which may lead to death." Unfortunately, that warning came too late.

The scandals linked to Indian factories are too numerous to count: employees of Ranbaxy Laboratories pleading guilty to making adulterated drugs in 2013; the bulk production and export of fake remdesivir (an antiviral) during COVID; Indian children fatally poisoned by cough syrup with high amounts of diethylene gycol; and another case that found not one but two different firms making fake diabetes drugs.[81]

"A report by United States Trade Representative (USTR) found that 20 percent of all pharmaceutical products sold on the Indian market are counterfeit," noted a 2022 article published by Deutsche Welle. "Official government records reveal that between 2007 and 2020, more than 7,500 drugs sampled in just three of India's 28 states and three union territories had failed quality tests. In 2018, the Central Drug Standard Control Organization identified about 4.5 percent of all generic drugs in the Indian market to be substandard. Furthermore, just one-fourth of the 12,000 manufacturing units in India were found to fulfill with the WHO's good manufacturing practices, the obligatory quality regulations that drug makers must adhere to."[82]

And those are just the ones we know about.

Second, the geopolitical question is as much a factor with India as it is with China. India has fraught relations with the United States. While nominally an ally, it is hardly a stalwart friend the way, for example, Poland or South Korea or Mexico is. Generally, Delhi and Washington are aligned on diplomatic affairs, but there have been some notable points of contention. Breaking from the U.S., other Western powers, and frankly most of the free world, India has taken a largely neutral stance on Russia's invasion of Ukraine, while increasing imports of Russian oil and fertilizer (actions which undermine Western sanctions against Russia).[83]

India's antidemocratic turn in recent years is also worrisome. The world's largest democracy, as it's often touted, is at risk of backsliding into authoritarianism. Its current president, Narendra Modi, leads the country with a brand of nationalism that puts him in the company of other "illiberal" leaders who play fast and loose with the norms of democratic government and jeopardize the very existence of the democratic system. Hostility to ethnic and religious minorities, a greater centralization of power, and curtailment of rights have been hallmarks of Modi's controversial rule.

On this point, we must acknowledge that the U.S. has, and does, actively cultivate alliances with terrible, autocratic countries where violating human rights seems like a national sport (e.g., Saudi Arabia). But generally, authoritarian states make poor bedfellows, and historically have been antagonistic toward the United States. An authoritarian India might find its values and aims align more closely with those of Russia or Iran, or even China (with whom it is a major trading partner). Do we really need to trade one totalitarian state for another as our nation's medical supplier?

Today the U.S. and India cooperate militarily, are active trade partners, have a shared interest in checking Chinese hegemony, and generally get along diplomatically, but that could all change in the years to come. India is, like all states, self-serving, and its warm relations with the United States will last only insofar as it's advantageous to maintain them. If Delhi decides it's strategically prudent to turn away from the West and toward Russia, Iran, or even an ascendant China (on which India depends for many of its imported goods—an unlikely but possible scenario), then the U.S. might find that the world's second-most-populous nation quickly devolves from friend to adversary.

I remember public opinion polls taken a decade ago about Americans' attitude toward China. Then, most Americans viewed China as a friend. Now, half of Americans consider China our greatest enemy.[84] Presently, most Americans have a favorable view of India, but I wonder if this trajectory will follow the same path as China: the high point before relations between our two countries erode, just as they have with China.

Finally, there is the unavoidable question of geography. At least until the tectonic plates hinge the subcontinent to California after a hundred million years, there is no getting around the fact that India is just too damn far. Transporting medical products over vast distances increases risk and cost, and inserts into the process a whole cast of middlemen—many sketchy, and all with their hand out—required to get something from Point A to Point B. Many things can go awry on the journey from Hyderabad to Oakland to Chicago. You don't really have that problem when you're making stuff in Akron or Phoenix.

Deceit, deception, embellishment, making false promises, graft, soul-crushing paperwork, contending with middlemen, inconsistency in word and deed, unpredictable results, and blatant, self-serving greed: this is the kind of thing you have to deal with when you procure medical supplies from India or China. It's like dealing with two used car salesmen who have car lots on opposite sides of the road, and America is just the hapless consumer in the middle, beholden to these two jokers, when all we're trying to do is buy a decent, reasonably priced sedan to drive our family around town.

Competition is usually good for the consumer, but in the next chapter, we'll discuss global competition in a pandemic world—and how the every-man-for-himself scramble for scarce drugs is good for no one.

CHAPTER 7

RUTHLESS COMPETITION IN A GLOBAL PANDEMIC

If you're running a factory and a man named Mr. Gold comes to you and tells you he's ready to buy what you're selling—a *lot* of it, in fact—and he has not only the funds, but the backing of the U.S. government, why would you object? Forget his unlikely, Bond villain-esque name. He's got the purchase order in hand! A contract for several million needles, signed and stamped by none other than the U.S. Department of Defense.

One afternoon, we got an email from our associates at Northfield relaying a message from one of our factories: *We receive email from Mr. Gold stating he now in charge of contract. Confirm this true. We begin moving inventory to his shipping company immediately* (sic).

Moreover, they said, Mr. Gold was armed with a copy of our federal contract. Whoever he was, he sure didn't work for us.

"Hold on," said Anthony. "Do you think he means 'Gold' as in 'Goldbelt, Inc.'?"

"Wait a minute. Do you mean like if some Chinese guy who couldn't really read English, or was running the contract through a low-grade translation app, mistook Goldbelt for the name of a person and it somehow got garbled into 'Mr. Gold'?"

We both laughed. It made perfect sense. It wasn't hard to obtain a copy of our contract with the DoD: all that information is publicly available information, if you know where to look (FOIA—thanks, G. Bush).

Anthony and I warned Northfield that Mr. Gold was not affiliated with iRemedy and was likely just another mercenary profiteer trying to lop off a piece of the COVID pie.

However, while we thwarted his scam, he managed to poison our well, because the situation further blunted the factory's trust in us. If you don't know who you can trust, you start mistrusting everyone—a situation exacerbated by the remote, digital nature of our relationship. Unfortunately, the lack of trust was mutual. By this point we didn't put a lot of stock in them either.

We never got to unmask the famous Mr. Gold, who disappeared once the scam fizzled out (with, I imagine, no consequences to him, as he presumably moved on to the next mark). Just one shark in a churning ocean teeming with thousands of them, emboldened by the chaos of the pandemic and the private and public money spigots that had been thrown open in its midst.

Other bad actors eschewed subterfuge in favor of the blunt force of capital. And for all its pretense of being a Marxist state, in China, money talks. You want people to move, you come with cash.

Or cars laden with gold bars.

In November 2020, Northfield tipped us off to another scam. Northfield had an employee on site at our largest factory who was monitoring production. Other sources informed us that she was probably carrying on an affair with a high-level official within that factory, but that's another story.

Thankfully, she took a break from her trysts with her paramour long enough to observe that agents of an unnamed Middle Eastern country had sent a car full of gold bullion to the site with the intention of bribing the right people into coughing up the inventory that belonged to us (and really, the American people.)

In Chinese factories, the chairman runs the show, and the local party bosses also have a stake, but a key figure is the person in charge of the factory loading dock. When I say "factory," don't picture some squat little building with a smokestack or two. Think of a massive manufacturing complex several city blocks long. That person arranges the arrival and departure of trucks. He's got power! He decides what shipments go out when, to whom, and what to do if "a crate falls off." And that's who the scammers attempted to sway.

That gambit didn't succeed either, but we knew that tomorrow, it would be someone else doing something equally outrageous. Competition for medical supplies was so fierce that every manner of con man, scammer, hustler, swindler, and impostor came out of the woodwork and jumped into the fray with the legitimate hospitals, health organizations, and national governments locking down medical supplies in preparation for the world's largest vaccination program, and it was often hard to distinguish the good guys from the bad ones. It was a no-holds-barred battle royale for needles and syringes, which had suddenly become some of the most coveted products in the world. And even though COVID has abated, the global market can still be a ruthlessly competitive place, which is part of the problem.

The Next Crisis

We were playing supply chain whack-a-mole: when you fix one problem, another one pops up.

While we fended off fraudsters and dealt with malfeasance at the site of production (all done in the fog of war, without really knowing what was actually happening on the ground), the problems with shipping and logistics persisted. After the empty flight debacle, the federal government hadn't formally absolved us, and we were still on the hook with Amerijet/TRANSCOM. They had proven themselves unfit for the job, but unfortunately, our contract obligated us to use them for eleven more flights. You might think, in a sane, logical world, that their obvious breach of duties would free us from obligation, but autumn 2020 was not a time where logic and sanity dictated the course of events. And even if we told Amerijet to kick rocks, where would that leave us? At square one again, with millions of needles piling up in China and no way of moving them.

We had little recourse but to close our eyes and hope for the best.

When it rains it pours, and when it pours, the deluge knocks your house off its foundation and carries it down river. That's pretty much where we were when the government threw us for a loop again.

In October 2020, the DoD changed the rules around which needles would be accepted for the OWS vaccination campaign. There are two general types used in medicine:

conventional needles, and safety needles. Safety needles retract, cover, or disarm the sharp point following the injection.

Originally, the contract was going to be a combination of safety and conventional needles. In a clinical setting, safety needles are not really necessary because the standard procedure is to immediately dispose of it in a sharps disposal container.

Now, the government was telling us, "We've got a new standard: we only want safety needles." We had already manufactured and delivered millions of conventional needles, with millions more coming down the assembly lines at the Chinese factories that we went to great lengths to hire. This unexpected and seemingly simple edict by the government would cause massive delays, tens of millions of dollars in losses, and haunt me for years to come.

Medically, on some level, the move made sense but in the context of everything else, it was a poor decision. There is nothing inherently "unsafe" about conventional needles. Even Joe Biden got vaccinated with one! Of course, we informed the DoD that this change would likely result in production delays and substantially raise costs, but our protests fell on deaf ears. They were intransigent.

Given the total lack of industrial flexibility in a world that seemed to be falling apart, coupled with the sky-high demand, we were in no position to go to the chairmen of the factories we hired and say, "Hey, about those needles—we changed our mind. Just give us safety needles, okay?" They had already bought raw materials, acquired molds for the machines, and tooled their equipment to churn out conventional needles. You don't just flip a switch; there are myriad "upstream" commitments that must be fulfilled and which preclude altering a big order. And if we tried to play hardball and threatened to refuse to pay them for the conventional needles, they would have just turned around and sold the product to someone else. Not to mention they had us on the hook for millions of dollars in deposits. We had no leverage.

Unsurprisingly, the factories flatly refused to accommodate us, so we were still on the hook for buying the conventional needles the factories in China had been contracted to produce, *plus* the added burden of having to scrounge up production capacity for three hundred million *extra* safety needles. To make matters worse, the world was on fire, with rabid demand worldwide for the same needles by every major country, all looking to source them from our small network of China-based factories.

The government was running out of patience and formally issued a "cure notice" letter, which basically demands that contractors prove they're doing what they're hired to do. They were making overtures about cutting us off. We had to talk them off the ledge.

Amerijet flew two successful flights in November. We hoped we could run out the clock with them on their contract and avoid additional disasters while we looked for an alternative transport option. Meanwhile, the holiday season was bearing down on us—when big brands ship huge volumes of goods from China to America—further putting a squeeze on supply chain logistics. COVID may have brought the world to its knees, but it would take nuclear war or the second coming of Christ to stop holiday shopping—and even then, it'll probably be billed as the "Apocalyptic Sales Event of the Season! Everything Must Go!"

Popular consumer electronics like the new Xbox, PlayStation, and iPhone were coming onto the market, and companies reserve logistics for big product rollouts years in advance, so we were up against that as well.

Our relationship with Amerijet/TRANSCOM ended, thankfully, on an anticlimactic note. We ran out the clock with them as they conducted the remaining flights uneventfully, and in December 2020, we struck a deal with Crane Worldwide Logistics to take over delivering the product from China to U.S. ports and trucking it from the ports to its destination.

Meanwhile, we were still constantly hounded by factories for additional deposits—always conveyed with the same extortionate tone and the same unrealistic timeline: pay up ASAP or we give your product to one of the hundred other buyers waiting in line. Four million dollars within seventy-two hours. Another sixteen million by next week. The beast's hunger for capital was voracious. My finance team, led by Amanda, and I spent hours on the phone with investors and banks to finance the deposits. It was reaching a breaking point, where we were becoming so severely overleveraged that the entire company might face a reckoning. You can only borrow so much before you're crushed under the weight of your debt.

The factories in China held all the cards, and they knew it. The entire American vaccination program was at the mercy of a few rapacious chairmen—and, above them, the Chinese Communist Party that pulls the strings and controls every facet of life and business in the Middle Kingdom.

For the first time, we were faced with a dilemma: maybe it was in the interest of the company, and our own sanity, to walk.

My wife's aunt was a nurse, one of the frontline health workers who were being celebrated by the public in those days. She contracted COVID, was hospitalized, and then recovered. Her release from the hospital was a joyous occasion. A colleague gave her a ride home, and as she was walking to her front door, she collapsed and died.

Then, the father of a partner of ours was infected and ended up on a ventilator, in isolation, since no one was allowed to see him. The virus ravaged his body until he could no longer put up a fight. He died alone and his loved ones had to say goodbye over a video call.

These were just a couple of the millions of tragic scenes playing out every day, usually beyond the view of the media and sometimes beyond the confines of an overwhelmed healthcare system. Not just death and illness but economic immiseration too, since entire industries had shut down and forced people out of work.

We just couldn't walk away from our commitment. We were duty-bound, no matter the cost or the risk.

No Control over Our Own Supply

As Anthony commutes by bike from his uptown apartment to our office downtown, he passes through Times Square, normally the busiest four square blocks in New York City, the capital of the world. In the early months of the pandemic, it was surreally deserted, its glowing signage blinking uselessly over eerily quiet streets devoid of cars, absent of people, drained of life. It felt apocalyptic.

Some semblance of normal life had resumed in the city by late 2020, but not because the U.S. had kept the virus at bay. On the contrary: as we entered the winter of 2020-2021, we were descending into the darkest period of the pandemic in terms of numbers of cases and deaths—"COVID hell," as Dr. Michael Osterholm, director of the Center of Infectious Disease Research and Policy at the University of Minnesota, put it.[85]

Anthony was inundated with calls that came in from unknown numbers—literally every fifteen minutes, usually people and organizations desperately seeking medical supplies. They had either found his cell phone number somewhere online or some contact had given it to them. He usually answered these mystery calls because you never knew who was on the other end.

Whether it was an urgent care facility in Kalamazoo or a regional hospital in Galveston, these calls all had a common trait: panic over the fact that their shelves were running bare and they had no way of replenishing their supplies. The illusion of control had vanished. It was something almost everyone took for granted before 2020. The underlying fragility of the supply chain had been hidden, like a crooked builder who paints over cracks in the foundation instead of fixing them.

And now, people were suffering.

One day, as Anthony was locking his bike up near the office, his phone rang. The woman identified herself as Lisa Noonemire, director of respiratory care at a small hospital in Kansas that operated elder care facilities. COVID's impact on nursing homes had been devastating. Until now, Lisa explained, the facilities under her care had avoided infection. But they'd just received their first case. She was in tears.

She needed ventilators and no one could help her, and she lacked the power to procure them.

Anthony told her he'd work on it and got off the phone. Then he turned to our local networks. The head of emergency supply I mentioned earlier—the one who called us distraught because the major urban hospital where he worked was running low on essential items—stepped up to help. He had dozens of surplus ventilators in reserved production. Anthony and I discussed the economics of brokering an arrangement to rent or sell Lisa some ventilators, but then we said, "Screw it, we're not taking money from this." Instead we just offered to connect her with our friend and let them work out something between them.

She was ecstatic and grateful—that was the best she could hope for. But dealing with these one-off problems was like fighting a Hydra. Cut off one head and two grow in its place.

Or, consider the harrowing testimony of a desperate ICU nurse, published in the *Journal of Pediatric Nursing*.[86]

> "It's hard to pick which was more dreadful, hearing the number of COVID patients in the Children's Hospital go up or hearing that we might run out of essential supplies that day. ... We were doing our best to care for fragile children, but it grew more challenging to keep our patients safe each day because of the lack of supplies. ... The lack of supplies was endangering our patients. We could not provide the care we owed to them. It resulted in so many kids getting worse."

These stories drove home the dire fact that even months into the pandemic—and still today—healthcare providers are at the mercy of the system. They have no control over their own supply. There was no Plan B. There still isn't. COVID did not create the problem; it just exacerbated it. Our healthcare system remains plagued by shortages. It's not just an abstract problem; the consequences are not mere inconvenience. People suffer and die.

Few people understand how vulnerable the American populace is better than David Sanders, who serves as VP of government affairs and policy for Coherus BioSciences and is executive director and founder of the Securing America's Medicines and Supply (SAMS) Coalition. The mission of SAMS Coalition (where I serve on the board of directors) is simple: "to strengthen the security of the medical supply chain in the United States . . . SAMS seeks to drive implementation of legislation and regulation to reward and foster U.S.-made manufacturing of important pharmaceutical products, devices, and personal protection equipment."[87]

Sanders has been sounding the alarm for years now and is working to call attention to the kind of shortages that go unnoticed by the press even though they may have deadly consequences. For example, a critical pediatric cancer drug that is only made in China is no longer available in the U.S. market, thanks to the lingering effects of COVID, China's strict lockdown policies, and other disruptions that have halted production.

If kids with cancer aren't enough reason to change the system, what is?

The list of drugs whose availability (as of this writing) is in jeopardy is not short: Tamiflu, amoxicillin, albuterol (a respiratory drug), and Adderall. A dearth of Pitocin (used to induce labor and treat bleeding from postnatal hemorrhages) has persisted for years.[88] A 2022 report from the National Academies of Sciences, Engineering, and Medicine found that while there aren't shortages across the board—and for some drugs, shortages have decreased in recent years—"Certain categories of drugs notably experience shortages more frequently than others," especially generics and particularly generic drugs that are older or low-priced, due to "lack of incentives to maintain adequate supply of low-margin drugs, low reimbursement rates, and market consolidation." Doctors perusing their storage rooms for anesthesia, antibiotics, nutrition and electrolyte products, and chemotherapy agents might find the shelves bare. Furthermore, "sterile injectable drugs are commonly in shortage, which may be explained by the manufacturing complexities and the high cost hurdle of entering the generic market."[89] The market is failing to meet demand.

Today, lack of raw materials and problems at the manufacturing site account for most of these disruptions. As we discussed before, a bottleneck can emerge at any point in the supply chain, from raw materials suppliers, to producers, to distributors, to providers. Transnational trade magnifies the risk and the impact of such bottlenecks, since every extra mile of transport, and every extra border and customs check, adds additional hurdles.

For medical products, as the National Academies report notes, each step in the supply chain is "usually operated by separate entities—often with multiple entities at some levels. This means that supply chains are not centrally controlled systems but are instead distributed networks with multiple decision makers that have different objectives. This can lead to mismatches in supply and demand, even under normal conditions."[90]

Demand surge (like we saw during COVID), capacity reduction (caused by labor shortages, war and geopolitical conflict, natural disasters, and other factors), and coordination failure (it's hard to get all the oars of a globalized boat rowing the same direction) are all triggers that can blow a fragile system apart.

It's not just needles and vaccines. The whole world is fighting over a limited number of vital medicines. When something comes up short, there is very little anyone can do—from the director of medical supplies to the hospital administrators to the doctors to the pharmacists, to you, the patient—except sit and wait. We have no control. This is not acceptable.

Meanwhile, a darker problem lurks beneath the surface. Even if you can get the medication you need, how do you know it's safe?

The truth is that you really don't.

The Role of the (Toothless) "Global FDA"

The FDA exists to ensure the medicine and food we put in our bodies won't harm us. While it does conduct limited oversight of factories abroad, it is dangerously inadequate. And sometimes the lack of oversight is fatal.

Heparin, an anticoagulant synthesized from pig intestines, is an essential and widely used drug, used to treat a variety of conditions, including heart attack and stroke. Unsurprisingly, China is the chief supplier of the world's, and

America's, heparin. In 2008, tainted heparin sourced from a Chinese factory and distributed by American pharmaceutical companies caused 350 adverse reactions and 150 deaths in the United States.[91]

The reason? After materials costs for heparin rose, the manufacturer searched for an alternative source, and added to its production process a cheap substitute (oversulfated chondroitin sulfate, or OCS) which cost one-tenth what the natural version did. Huge batches of heparin were shipped worldwide from China, cut with the soon-to-be fatal adulterant, like a heroin dealer cutting his product with rat poison before it hits the streets.

One hundred fifty Americans died and hundreds became ill before the toxic batches were pulled. Illnesses and deaths were also reported in other countries. It was an outrage—and one of the rare moments when the issue of foreign medical suppliers drew public scrutiny.

Baxter International and Scientific Protein Laboratories (SPL), the American companies that had contracted Chinese factories to produce heparin, were summoned to Capitol Hill to testify. It isn't often that such issues draw the attention of Congress—but when there are fatalities, people take notice. The FDA was also taken to task in public hearings. Shockingly, as Gibson and Singh note in *China RX*, "FDA officials revealed during the hearings that the SPL plant in China had never been inspected because an FDA employee had mistakenly clicked on the wrong company name from a drop-down menu on the computer and inadvertently requested an inspection of a different plant. Both Baxter and SPL knew the FDA hadn't inspected it but sold products made in the plant anyway."[92]

So while the FDA flubbed the inspection, why did the companies themselves not know what was going on at the plants they had contracted? As it turns out, they were barely monitoring what was happening at the production site. They tested every lot of heparin that arrived stateside, but the tests were not designed to detect the particular contaminant that sickened and killed so many people.[93] Nor were they even able to locate the precise source of the contamination. And it would have been difficult if not impossible to link a specific batch to the Chinese pig farm where it originated.[94]

The means by which heparin, like other drugs, is produced for the market is rather messy and lacks transparency. "Consolidators collect crude heparin lots, combine them, and sell them to manufacturers (or to brokers to sell to manufacturers) to produce active pharmaceutical ingredients (APIs) . . . In China, not all heparin makers are overseen by drug regulators, because some are registered as chemical makers."[95]

The reality is that no one—not the pharmaceutical companies, not the distributors, not the FDA, and certainly not the doctors and nurses administering these drugs—really knows where they come from, what kind of facilities they're processed in, what the sources of the raw materials are, and whether the manufacturers are skirting regulations, cutting corners, and ignoring health and safety standards. The heparin tragedy of 2008 was an egregious example, and not the only one. Worse, it's only a matter of time before it happens again.

If you're making a device or drug, you must be certified by FDA. They dispatch a team of inspectors and go over your facility with a fine-toothed comb. But how can they oversee a factory three thousand miles inland in China in some remote and inaccessible city? Many of China's industrial centers are in the middle of nowhere. Getting to them can be like climbing Mount Doom in J.R.R. Tolkien's *Lord of the Rings*.

The FDA lacks the manpower and resources to adequately surveil the facilities where the lifesaving drugs we give our kids and elderly parents and ourselves are being fabricated. It costs about twice as much to inspect a foreign plant as it does a domestic one.[96] As Gibson and Singh write, "Unlike a poorly made shirt whose seams begin to fray after a few spins in the washing machine, the consumer can't tell if a pill is well-made by looking at it. Doctors and the public assume the federal government was enforcing drug safety standards for all medicines. But the FDA didn't have the authority to enforce the gold standard of drug manufacturing Americans had come to expect."[97]

In theory, more Congressional funding would allow the agency to cast a wider net overseas, hiring and training the necessary personnel and funding their trans-Pacific expeditions. But it's not only a matter of mustering more financial resources. Inspecting factories in China and India and elsewhere has all kinds of logistical and cultural hurdles that more funding won't fix.

First, surprise inspections of a factory would be preferable, but the FDA's visits are planned well in advance. China doesn't take too kindly to agents of a foreign government (especially those of the United States) showing up unannounced at its production facilities. And that gives factories the opportunity to clean up their act and put the necessary window dressing on their pharmaceutical Potemkin villages to appease the FDA agents.

Even if China were to give the FDA carte blanche to visit whenever, wherever, it just wouldn't make sense. Factories do not operate 24/7/365; they sometimes shut down due to mechanical breakdown, natural disaster, public holidays, or other reasons. Imagine spending thousands in taxpayer dollars to send a team of inspectors abroad, only for them to press their bespectacled faces against the locked, glass front doors as they ask, "Is anybody home?"

So these checks almost certainly have to be conducted with prior notice and approval.

Culture and language gaps are also a factor. This involves a lot more than just learning a few greetings in Mandarin or knowing when to bow and when to shake hands. Navigating cultural and, especially, language disparities puts a strain on even the most proficient American agent. Inspectors not only need to communicate orally; they also need to comb through pages (sometimes many) of technically complex documentation. Clear communication and transparency are paramount in the business of inspection. But that breaks down when you don't share a common language, even when you have the help of a skilled interpreter or translator. When the linchpin of that process is a translator—in all likelihood a local, whom you may or may not trust and whose credentials you may or may not be able to verify—even the most diligent inspector's ability to work freely is stymied. It is not uncommon for agents of foreign suppliers to use the language and cultural differences to their advantage as they negotiate in the sometimes murky world of international trade.

"Virtual inspections" conducted remotely are a possible solution, one we'll explore later in the book, but so far, the government has not authorized agents to replace or supplement in-person inspections with virtual ones, and it's unclear if the Chinese would allow it.

One can also make the case that as a watchdog agency, the FDA itself is structurally flawed. I know I'm not the first person to raise this argument—Americans tend to have strong, often hostile feelings toward "Big Pharma," and the suspicion that the agency that regulates it has been "captured" by large drug manufacturers is not entirely unfounded. In truth, the FDA receives 45 percent of its budget from "industry user fees" paid by drug companies when a new drug application is filed.[98] There are advantages and disadvantages to this arrangement. But whenever one entity is dependent upon another for its funding, it creates the potential for a conflict of interest.

So if FDA inspections of Chinese facilities were scant *before* COVID, you can imagine what happened when the pandemic erupted. Air travel declined and borders closed. China, not exactly an "open" country to begin with, yanked up the drawbridge and walled itself off from the rest of the world.

That was the environment we had to deal with when the government called an audible on the type of needle they wanted for OWS. We had to race to find additional factories that could handle the uptick in production, and these new factories *also* had to be approved by the FDA. But inspectors weren't allowed in. So we had to fight with Chinese officials to obtain documentation, certification, photographs, and samples, which we then turned over to the FDA, in order to get approval to use these factories as a source. In fact, we had to cancel a couple of flights because we didn't have enough inventory to fill them since the approvals were pending. Though it was beyond our control, it just encouraged further accusations that we were underperforming and flubbing the whole thing.

We even offered to fly over there ourselves and conduct an inspection personally. In locked-down China this was almost impossible, but we were able to finagle a compromise—they were willing to issue us a special visa, with one big caveat: officially, we would be classified as flight crew members, and we wouldn't be permitted to leave the plane, so we couldn't actually visit the production site. What would have been the point of that? Then they offered an equally unworkable "compromise": we could leave the plane, but we'd be quarantined in our hotel room. It was absurd.

It's also worth talking about the FDA's faulty 510(k) system. Section 510(k) of the Food, Drug, and Cosmetic Act governs the agency's approval of medical device production, at home and abroad. A 510(k) letter is the certification/permit that grants you license to produce a product for the U.S. market. It's a big deal to get your 510(k). If you don't have it, you can't import your product into the U.S.

But we have observed through our own dealings in China that factory owners play games with 510(k) clearances, basically letting other manufacturers use their own 510(k) letter—for a fee, of course—in order to manufacture goods that bear the imprimatur of FDA approval.

It works like this: say I have a factory in Stuart, Florida that makes tennis shoes. Anthony has a 510(k)-approved factory in New York that makes needles and syringes. I want to get in on the lucrative needle game, but the FDA says, "Nope, sorry, not without a 510(k) clearance." So, knowing that the FDA is never going to grant it for my tennis shoe factory, I cut a deal with

Anthony: "Let us manufacture needles, stamp it with your factory's seal using your 510(k), and you get a slice of the profits." The only victim here is, of course, the FDA, and by extension, the American consumer put at risk by medical devices being made in unapproved factories. This idea would never fly in the United States, but China is a different story.

This practice is so widespread and brazen that no one really tries to hide it, and during COVID, it was even worse. It was like an elementary school classroom where the teacher leaves a room full of unruly children. In the absence of federal supervision, every factory owner was telling us, "Well, we don't have a 510(k), but our sister factory in Lanzhou does." What does "sister factory" even mean? Nothing, for all intents and purposes, except a marriage of convenience between two profiteers. And in theory, they're all "sister factories" because they're all owned by the CCP. But that doesn't mean they all adhere to the same stringent standards.

By the end of 2020, we were stuck between two slow-moving giants, one in the U.S., the other in China. That's the nature of the global FDA, which offers the worst of both worlds, both "too much" and "too little": a slow, inefficient approvals process and patchy, incomplete oversight.

Blood in the Water: The Feeding Frenzy

The absence of oversight or accountability in a free-for-all global marketplace begat scam after scam after scam.

One day our main factory received a call from a "Mary Davidson," wanting to buy our allocation. Unlike Mr. Gold, Mary is a real person; we know because she worked for us! She used to be iRemedy's purchasing director before moving onto another role at the company. She doesn't deal with the factories directly. So when the factory notified us that they had been in touch with Mary, we suspected it wasn't *our* Mary, but just another two-bit hustler who had found her name somewhere online.

Just to confirm, I asked her, "Hey, Mary, have you been talking to factories in China?"

"What?! I didn't talk to a factory in China. Or any factory!"

That was one of the more common schemes: random impostors misrepresenting their relationships with either buyers or sellers. The impact was doubly inauspicious because not only did we have to fend off bad actors trying to muscle in on our product, the constant acts of fraud leached trust out of the market, so legitimate companies we wanted to work with were often suspicious of *us*. Suppliers didn't believe that I was the head of an established medical supply company. A couple times, I had to send "proof of life," like in a kidnapping, and take a picture in front of our warehouse holding that day's newspaper.

Nothing could be taken at face value and no one's word meant anything because you never really knew who you were dealing with on the other end of a WhatsApp call or email.

Sometimes, it wasn't so much an act of deliberate fraud as incompetence, usually in the form of overpromising and failing to deliver. So many players with zero experience in the industry jumped into the fray. They were just responding to torrid demand, and thought they could broker deals between buyers and suppliers. This only served to muddy the waters. It was hard to distinguish the legitimate actors from the overconfident opportunists and ruthless con artists. And that confusion was, don't forget, amplified by twelve-hour time zone differences, language barriers, and cultural misunderstandings.

Now, one could perhaps say that these circumstances were exceptional; that COVID's climate of chaos and desperation made fraud so rampant. Or that scammers operate in the U.S. too and domesticating production doesn't eliminate that risk. Both those statements are true, to an extent. But the farther you situate the site of production from the end user—far beyond the legal protections afforded by the United States, with manifold borders, legal jurisdictions, and middlemen between factory and patient—the more onerous things will become and the more competition, theft, and flouting of safety standards in the Wild West of the open market will degrade healthcare professionals' ability to serve people in need.

The next chapter simulates in war-game detail what might happen when day-to-day burdens of the supply chain blow up into an actual crisis—the human toll that is wrought when medicine is weaponized during an open conflict between the United States and China, a nightmare scenario that is becoming more probable with each passing day.

CHAPTER 8

A WAR GAME FOR A DANGEROUS NEW WORLD

A war game is a military training exercise used to sharpen fighting forces' readiness, simulate on-the-ground events that might transpire during an actual conflict, and identify "blind spots" in strategy and tactics. Years ago—as a technology industry leader—I attended a Naval War College event where we were briefed on the role of technology in global warfare, and they took us through several "war game" scenarios. During my role in Operation Warp Speed, I realized that we were living out a scenario that should have been "war gamed."

The following is a fictional account—based in fact and informed by actual "war game" simulations conducted by think tanks and the U.S. military—of what could (and likely would) happen if the nightmare scenario of China weaponizing the American medical supply transpired. It's not just a narrative interlude for the reader's amusement (indeed, at heart, there is nothing "amusing" about it), but rather a sober, blow-by-blow study of probable outcomes and an exposé of the public health, economic, and national security vulnerabilities addressed in the preceding chapters. While previous war games have closely examined military maneuvers, none, to our knowledge, has incorporated this consideration in their analysis.

1. Taipei, Taiwan: June 25

The skyscrapers of the bustling Taiwanese capital gleamed in the sunlight. At ground level, ripples of excitement reverberated through a crowd gathered outside the Hotel de Chine, where Mei-Ling Zhang, the leading presidential candidate for the upcoming January elections, was making an appearance.

Zhang was as electrifying as she was polarizing; she and her upstart party had jolted the presidential race. She was doing what no other frontrunner had done: promising to reunify Taiwan with the People's Republic of China. It had always been a contentious position in Taiwan, where most people still favored independence, but she had shocked pundits, the public, and the world by surging ahead.

Everyone feared that a Chinese invasion would spell the demise of Taiwan as a de facto free nation (whether Taiwan was a state unto itself depended on whom you asked.) But few had imagined that it might happen electorally.

The threat—or the opportunity, depending on your perspective—was coming from the inside.

Ten-year-old Chih-weh held his father's hand as the crowd pressed around them, waiting. But all he could see from his vantage point was a tangle of legs. His father was a supporter of Zhang. His mother, who had grudgingly agreed to attend, was stridently opposed. But mostly, they brought their son to witness something exciting. Perhaps, in Zhang's candidacy, they were seeing history in the making, for better or worse.

Inside the hotel, Zhang strode through the lobby with her entourage, her ample security team, and the gaggle of reporters that followed her everywhere.

No one would have seen the powerful explosive device hidden inside a sculpture in the lobby.

In a flash, the opulent hotel lobby turned into a horror scene as the bomb ripped through Zhang's entourage, killing a dozen. Mei-Ling Zhang bled out on the carpet.

Chi-weh and his parents were a hundred yards from the roped-off entrance, but they heard the blast over the crowd noise. It didn't immediately register what the sound was, but a surge of panic and chaos rapidly spread from the carnage inside the entrance, outward to the crowd, like a tidal wave.

As the spectators closest to the entrance turned and fled, a stampede ensued. Chi-weh's father grabbed his son and his wife as they raced to safety.

They didn't know what had happened, but they would always remember this moment in searing detail. The instant when their country, and the world, irreversibly changed.

2. Kaiser Permanente, Reston, Virginia, June 25

"In summary, there's good news and bad news, but mostly good," said Dr. Charles. The young oncologist had an easygoing, gentrified Southern manner, but he was terse and to the point. "The bad news is that the cancer has not responded to treatment. The good news is that vincristine is an excellent drug with a high rate of effectiveness. Kids in Leah's condition generally respond well to it. There are side effects, yes. And she'll be in the hospital for most of what we call the induction phase.

That's about five weeks. But then, in all likelihood, she'll be released."

John and Carol Carter, both forty-two, sat side by side, listening intently. The diagnosis of pediatric cancer in their only child Leah, age nine, had devastated them. Since that moment, their lives had been a whirlwind of clinic visits, obscure medical terminology, treatment options, specialists, and moments of hope that briefly interrupted a gnawing sense of dread. Leah herself had taken the news rather stoically. Nine-year-olds don't always grasp the enormity of death. She understood she was very sick. But she held strong.

Carol spoke up. "You said the prognosis is favorable, right?"

"Very," the doctor said. "It's the best drug we have right now."

John's phone, until then dead weight in his hands, buzzed alive with the arrival of a text message. Carol flashed him a disapproving look ("work can wait"), and he muttered, "Sorry." But as he moved to shut the phone off, something caught his eye. The message was "tagged" with a code that CIA agents knew meant urgent. As a senior analyst in the CIA, he knew this was no ordinary work communication.

Then it rang.

"Apologies, I think I have to take this."

"John, really?" said his wife. But the look in his eye told her it was serious.

John opened the text. Zhang assassinated. Briefing in one hour. We need you there.

* * *

John and Carol made their way through the waiting room of the hospital, which was packed with sick people. The flu this season was a particularly virulent strain and had already reached epidemic levels—not as devastating as the COVID-19 pandemic, but the toll was creeping ever upward, straining health systems and putting a squeeze on vital drugs. Still, barring some local shortages here and there, people were getting the treatment, and the drugs, they needed.

Across the room, by the sliding glass doors, John's father, Harold, seventy-five, waited with Leah. He doted endlessly on his only grandchild and had been a rock of support through this ordeal, despite his own health problems.

Most patients were staring into their phones as they waited. With breathless urgency, some were riveted by the breaking story broadcast on the cable news station on the waiting room TV. The correspondent rehashed the bare facts over images of the destruction in the lobby, and the fleeing crowds outside.

Within minutes, the incident in Taipei had become a global story. John watched a clip that would remain seared in the world's collective consciousness, one he'd see many times over the next weeks, often drifting up into his dreams. The last images of Zhang, one second at the pinnacle of her career, gliding through the lobby to greet her supporters; the next, human flesh turned to bits of bone and muscle. Human life dissolved into air . . .

One question hung in the air like the smoke lingering from the explosive: Who did this?

3. Zhongnanhai, Beijing, China, June 25

"Who did this?" Guo Shen thundered from a secure office deep underground in the Zhongnanhai compound, the headquarters of the Chinese Communist Party. "I want answers!"

As CCP general secretary and president of the People's Republic, the unbearable weight of decision fell on his shoulders. But they were all moving through a fog of war.

"We're racing to figure that out, sir," said Li Tang, head of China's Ministry of State Security.

"You should have known within ten minutes!"

The assassination prompted an immediate gathering of China's top leaders, just as similar scenes played out among heads of state everywhere. Every second mattered and every decision could have consequences that would ripple throughout the world. But no one knew anything.

"We knew she was at risk. We picked up a lot of chatter involving threats against her life in the recent weeks. But nothing material," said Tang.

"What chatter? It was all over the internet! Any idiot could have seen that she was in danger! You're supposed to be intelligence agents. Tell us something the whole world doesn't already know."

The Minister of National Defense, Ho-san Bow, spoke up. "Our working theory is that the operation was carried out by a sleeper cell of Taiwanese nationalists backed by the United States."

"Who is 'our'?" said Tang. "We don't know anything yet and I object to any premature conclusion. The truth is, it could have been any number of entities. The United States, or operatives working on behalf of the United States. The UBG. One of these radical student groups that's been protesting at every campaign stop. A lone wolf citizen trying to push the wheel of history on his own. Someone in the DPP," he said, referring to one of Taiwan's main political parties, and Zhang's campaign rivals. "Even a jealous ex-lover."

"Is that supposed to be funny?"

"No, sir," Tang said dryly. "I'm simply stressing that she had made many enemies."

"How we respond is the more pressing matter," said the defense minister.

"How can we respond if we don't know who the guilty party is?" Tang countered.

"No, he's right," said Shen. "Inaction now would be fatal."

"Sir, I caution you not to respond with haste. I don't need to tell you what kind of consequences the wrong move could bring."

4. White House, Washington, DC, June 25

Meanwhile, seven thousand miles away, White House officials were also racing to mount a response.

President Rhodes, not one for emergency meetings in the early morning, rubbed his tired eyes. This was the nightmare scenario they had long feared—one they had certainly planned for, but planning is one thing, action another.

Also present were Melissa Mills, CIA director; Javier Dario, the secretary of state; General Richard Amdur, chairman of the Joint Chiefs of Staff (CJCS); and a few other members of the Cabinet.

Mills finished her briefing. "So in summary, as I said, it's too soon to make a firm determination. But our intel suggests that this was a false flag operation by the CCP to serve as a pretext for a Taiwanese invasion."

"And are they invading?"

"There's been a flurry of military action already. Two warships are steaming toward Taipei. A battalion is being mobilized in Shanghai and Shenzhen."

"Doesn't necessarily indicate a pretext," Rhodes said. "That's what they would rationally do if they suspect, as I imagine they do, that we were behind the assassination." He paused. "And a false flag doesn't make sense to me. We've known for years that Beijing prefers unification by means other than war. And Zhang's campaign was perhaps their best shot."

Mills said, "Yes, it would be a risky maneuver, and out of character. But I need not remind you that states do not always act rationally. The graveyard of history is full of leaders who blundered their way into a fight they couldn't win. It's also possible that it was a rogue operative within the CCP; someone acting unilaterally, without Guo Shen's blessing."

The general, a granite statue of silence until now, rose. "The more important question is how do we respond. At the least, I suggest a partial mobilization of the Seventh Fleet. A partial mobilization. Move Destroyer Squadron 5 from Yokosuka toward the north coast of Taiwan. Let the carriers hold back, for now. Let's show strength, but avoid aggressive posturing."

"Where the hell is the Chinese ambassador?" said Rhodes.

"Beijing has not responded to our communications. And the Embassy has issued no statement," Mills said.

"Either they're freezing us out—or they're just as in the dark as we are and are afraid of doing or saying the wrong thing."

"Indeed, Mr. President. It could be either."

The president was seized by a coughing fit that rattled his lungs and made him wheeze.

"You all right, sir?" asked Mills.

"Yes, yes, excuse me," the president said. "Goddamn flu."

5. Pacific Ocean/South China Sea, June 27

In Chinese mythology, Longwang—the Dragon King— dominates the seas. The fearsome Longwang is sometimes depicted as a scowling human warrior, sometimes as a mighty reptilian beast. Aggressive and temperamental, he reigns over the seas.

If the mythic creature was made real—scales and flesh turned to steel and fire—it might have looked like China's thousand-foot-long Shandong aircraft carrier as it powered through the choppy Pacific waters. Accompanied by destroyers, cruisers, and a phalanx of submarines, there was nothing but sea and sky between the fleet and the Taiwanese shores, just a hundred miles from mainland China.

The blockade had begun.

The CCP president had made the order after weighing the recommendations of his hawkish defense minister and his more cautious state security minister. A blockade was, he and his advisers reasoned, the best course of action, a risky, but rational, midpoint between full-on invasion and standing down militarily. Invasion was still on the table, but an incursion of Taiwan by air and ground forces would, all likely scenarios suggested, come at an immense cost, even if the United States did not come to the aid of its island ally. Taiwanese forces were well equipped and had trained for years for this crisis. And if the U.S. did commit its forces—well, that would all but ensure a bloodbath for both sides, if not World War III.

A blockade had other advantages: it could be de-escalated or reversed should the gambit prove counterproductive. And it would avoid mass casualties for the Taiwanese people, whom China sought to integrate, rather than conquer—a unified China, correcting the decades-old splintering of the "two Chinas" since Chiang Kai-shek crossed the strait and founded Taiwan.

No one in the Chinese state had confirmed who killed Zhang or whether America's hands were bloody. But as the more cunning advisers in Guo Shen's circle noted, it did not matter: all that mattered was that the world believed China believed the U.S. was at fault. That gave China some much-needed leverage.

Meanwhile, China's global diplomatic and media apparatus went into overdrive "selling" the blockade as a defensive act to protect the Taiwanese people. The Chinese representative at the U.N. gave a statement to the Security Council. Chinese-friendly media, meanwhile, were pushing the narrative hard that this was not an act of aggression but a reasonable, measured response to what was in all likelihood (so they said) yet another incident of the CIA lethally intervening in another nation's politics.

The steel behemoths on the water's surface were imposing, but the greater menace skulked beneath the waters. China was using its state-of-the-art attack submarines as the tip of the spear. The subs would be less vulnerable to U.S. missiles, but still capable of encircling Taiwan, and keeping foreign ships—military and civilian alike—far away.

China had sixty subs at the ready; forty were deployed in the blockade, armed with both torpedoes and antiship missiles.99 The Chinese naval commander was given clear orders about the rules of engagement: any ship that attempted to bypass the blockade would be fired upon. Privately, Politburo leaders prayed that this would not come to pass. Sinking another state's vessel would almost surely widen the war and commit China to a course of action it did not wish to pursue. But the blockade would only succeed if the threat of force was backed with action.

The Chinese fleet fanned out throughout the waters surrounding Taiwan, blocking shipping lanes and laying sea mines. With the American fleet still some distance away, China managed to choke off the island's maritime trade in days, without firing a shot.

For decades, the U.S. had walked a tightrope on the Taiwan issue, deftly crafting a policy of "strategic ambiguity" that would leave China with no clarity about how Washington would respond to Chinese aggression in or around Taiwan. Unlike the NATO treaty that bound the U.S. to defend its allies if any NATO member was attacked, there was no such written commitment with Taiwan.

Making overtures toward military defense without formally committing to outright defense let the U.S. keep China at bay while preserving all possible options. For a long time, this ambiguity was an effective deterrent, inhibiting China's ability to gauge a U.S. response.

Until now. The moment Chinese ships surged into Taiwanese waters—Longwang wrapping its serpentine body around Taiwan's neck, and squeezing—China was effectively calling America's hand. Was the U.S. promise to keep Taiwan free all bluff and bluster? The world watched and waited.

6. Linney Pharmacy, Reston, Virginia, June 30

Talk of armed conflict dominated the headlines, family breakfast conversations, water-cooler chats, and the TV and radio waves across America. Even those who rarely paid attention to global events sat up and took notice. America and China were in a dangerous standoff. When you went to bed at night, you weren't sure if you'd wake up the next morning to news that the standoff had escalated into war. The conflict was centered on the other side of the globe, but it suddenly felt very near. And imminent.

Harold Brown was one of those folks who didn't concern himself much with foreign events, foreign policy, or politics in general. Not that he didn't care, but at seventy-five years old, he had seen it all, and he preferred to focus on his own environment—the things he could control, the things he could touch and see. Since his wife, John's mother, had died eight years prior, his family—John, Carol, and Leah—was his whole world.

That morning, Harold stood in line at Linney Pharmacy, beneath the hum of fluorescent lights and the tinny sound of Top 40 on the drugstore's PA system, waiting to pick up his heparin, a blood thinner medication. Several million Americans depended on the drug, which had been in short supply over the past year—"supply chain issues" being the vague explanation. "Give me a boat and I'll bring over the damn stuff myself," Harold had joked. He didn't understand why they couldn't get it right. But he had been lucky. Chuck Linney, whose family ran the store, always stocked what he needed. He had heard stories of other seniors like him who had to drive two states over to find a pharmacy that would fill the prescription.

"Hey, Howard, good to see ya," Linney called out to him. Howard had been lost in thought and hadn't seen the last customer before him depart.

"Hey, Chuck," he said. "You got my prescription in the system?"

"Howard, you ask the same thing every time," the white-coated pharmacist chuckled.

"Old dog, new tricks. Or something like that."

"Believe me, I hear ya."

Linney tapped away on his computer. His brow furrowed and his eyes flashed a hint of worry behind his thick spectacles.

"Well, hold on a minute," said Linney. "Can't seem to find you in the system. Might have to reboot. Hey, how's your granddaughter doing?"

"She's okay, thanks for asking. They're putting her on a new drug. Hopefully this one works."

"Amen," Linney said. Then, still eyeing the screen: "Goddamn it. Forgive my language. Computer isn't cooperating today." He turned toward his young Bangladeshi colleague in the back. "Farouk, your computer working?"

"It just stopped."

Linney tapped the keys in frustration. "Well, now the whole system is down!"

Farouk came to the front. "I just got an email. Walgreens and Rite-Aid are down too. There are outages in pharmacy chains all over the country."

Howard cleared his throat. "I hate to be a bother, but I really need that medication."

"I know, Howard, and I'm real sorry, but we can't fill the prescription until the system is back up. Should just be a blip. Can you come back this afternoon?"

7. Taipei, Taiwan, June 30

Chih-weh sat at the kitchen table in their cramped, twenty-fourth-story two-bedroom apartment as his parents took stock of the contents of their kitchen cabinet. Storage space was small and the family ate most meals out, or relied on the dizzying array of takeout options. This was the first time he saw them stockpile food.

Normally, hundreds of ships entered Taiwan's ports each day. But with the Chinese armada lurking in the seas, that number had been reduced to a dozen. The blockade wasn't absolute, but it was effective. Yesterday, a merchant vessel was torpedoed on the west side of the island. The ship was immobilized but didn't sink. But the warning shot was enough to signal to shipping companies and seamen worldwide: cross the line at your own peril.

China's naval action had sent Taiwan into a panic. Taiwan's military went into full alert mode. Reservists, including Chih-weh's own father, had been called up. Civilians scrambled to stockpile food, medicine, hygienic products—all the day-to-day items they had been accustomed to having in abundance. Shortages were all but guaranteed, despite the government's pleas for calm.

His mother, seeing the look of worry on the young boy's face, reassured him. "Don't worry, son. This is going to pass soon."

Chih-weh took a look at the food they had. A few bags of rice, some canned vegetables, noodles. Not much else. Even at his age, he did the math: three people, three meals a day (if the restaurants stopped operating)—it wasn't much.

8. Herndon, Virginia, July 1

On a humid afternoon, John Brown drove along Elden Street on the way to work. He idly scanned the radio stations before settling on talk radio: some loudmouthed war hawk calling for the U.S. to launch a naval attack in the Pacific and bomb the Chinese mainland. Good thing he's on the radio and not in the Pentagon, thought John. But then, he wondered how many hawks in the government or military were unwisely yearning for the same thing.

You didn't have to be a CIA analyst to understand a war with China was almost surely a lose-lose proposition. Any victory would be Pyrrhic, at best. It would be so devastating, it would hardly be a victory at all. And that was a best case. The worst case, it wasn't hyperbolic to think, would be civilization-ending catastrophe.

But then, what to do? This was the kind of national security conundrum that kept heads of states and their advisers up at night—a complicated, multifaceted problem with sky-high stakes and few options. Each path would incur a great risk, great loss. Armed conflict in defense of Taiwan? You were gambling on WWIII, even a nuclear exchange. Unfathomable. On the other hand, should the U.S. just stand down and let China strangle

Taiwan with an illegal blockade? The U.S. wouldn't just lose an ally, it would lose face; it would put all its alliances at risk. And the world, the free world, needed Taiwan's semiconductor industry to function.

That day, John was being summoned to brief CIA Director Mills. Though just an analyst, he was recognized within the agency as an expert in China—one of the few who actually spoke fluent Mandarin.

John turned off the radio. He had heard enough. He passed the familiar sights of suburban DC: strip malls, middle schools with manicured lawns, unassuming family-owned Indian and Vietnamese restaurants, the Salvadoran chicken place he took his kid to after softball games. A calm and placid way of life, now gravely at risk. He wondered if his Chinese counterpart was thinking the same. They were rivals on two sides of a grievous conflict, and yet they weren't all that different.

Up ahead, traffic had snarled to a standstill. He moved along at a crawl. Traffic jams were hardly unheard of even here in the suburbs, but at this hour, it was unusual. Then he saw the reason: the streetlights were out, and the intersection had devolved into chaos, underscored by an unpleasant symphony of car horns.

Then he realized the lights everywhere in the neighborhood were out.

And if he had kept the radio on, he might have heard the news from the Midwest, South, and West Coast: there were mysterious power outages being reported all over the country.

East China Sea, July 2

WAR GAME

The hulking mass of gray steel listed at a nauseating angle, battered by the waves. The South Korean merchant ship, which had crisscrossed the Pacific twenty times in its lifetime, had made its last voyage. It was, unfortunately, now the most famous ship in the world: the latest flashpoint in the escalating global conflict.

A Chinese naval mine had blown a hole in its hull. Chinese subs had laid the mines in a ring along the perimeter of the island, at the approach to its major ports, and made their presence (if not their exact location) known to the world. In war, every measure has a countermeasure, and normally, the U.S. would deploy its naval minesweeping faculties to clear the mines. But doing so would put its forces within close range of Chinese carriers and destroyers.

Eight of the twenty-three crew members on board lost their lives. The deceased were citizens of six nations, all of which protested vociferously but had no real means of retaliation. Instead, they looked to the U.S. to act. That the vessel flew the flag of South Korea, a close East Asian ally, increased the pressure on the Americans to act.

A near-universal United Nations condemnation of the blockade had not overcome Chinese resolve. The CCP had known all along their actions would incur the wrath of the global community. Guo Shen and the rest of the Politburo inner circle felt that after decades of biding their time, China was powerful enough to act unilaterally. They just had to ride it out. It was a matter of seeing who blinked first.

Chinese and American authorities had been in constant negotiations, and the U.S. government attempted to use what leverage it had, but neither moral suasion, nor promised economic sanctions, nor the threat of a complete trade embargo with China convinced Beijing to call their ships back to port.

Meanwhile, President Rhodes fended off calls from hawks in the Pentagon, Congress, and even in his own administration to take the war to launch strikes on the blockading ships or even attack the Chinese mainland. As Rhodes sat at his Oval Office desk, head in his hands, he thought about what President Kennedy, sitting in this very spot, must have gone through during the Cuban Missile Crisis, as he agonized over his options. Then, too, hawkish elements were pushing Kennedy to bomb Cuba, and Kennedy demurred.

Finally, twenty-four hours after the mine incident, the White House and joint chiefs agreed on a response. It was time to break the blockade. Just like in the Cuban Missile Crisis, the hope was that the threat of force, and the presence of the superior American fleet, would be enough to force the Chinese to back off. No one wanted a shooting war. The mission was just to open up a shipping lane, not only to provide immediate relief for the people of Taiwan, but to signal that the Chinese attempt would be unsuccessful. If the U.S. Navy could get a foothold, and hold that lane, it might be enough.

* * *

Despite its highly classified nature, it was one of those meetings where history was made. Scholars and experts would debate and dissect it for years.

The American president listened as CJCS Amdur explained, "Our best chance for breaking the blockade is to bring to bear enough forces to force the Chinese to back off the west coast of Taiwan. Kaoshiung is the island's most critical port, and that, along with Taipei, is, for now, inaccessible. But the port of

Hualien is in play. In concert with Japan, if we can create a lane extending several hundred miles from the coast, we can open that port."

"And what will that require?"

"The operation will be relatively limited in the scale of force involved. The minimum necessary to overcome resistance, we reason. It is not 'shock and awe.' It's measured. Contained."

"It has to be," the president said.

"Japan has agreed to let us use our bases there as a base of operations. But they will not dispatch any of their forces."

"That is unfortunate."

"They are steadfast. This is the middle-of-the-road approach for them, between neutrality and shooting at the Chinese. It's the best we can do."

George Bush Center for Intelligence (CIA Headquarters), Langley, Virginia, July 4

His bosses had greeted the news of the successful U.S. operation with self-congratulatory fanfare. John avoided the celebration, which he worried was premature, and a little myopic. Yes, the U.S. had managed to carve out a shipping lane on the east side of the island. China still had a grip on the rest of the island, but it was a victory for the U.S. Still, had the intelligence community learned nothing from Iraq, Afghanistan, and other hasty, overly optimistic assessments of their power?

In his heart, John knew, with great trepidation, that whether or not the U.S. "won" this conflict—and it was hard to even say what winning looked like—the previous era was done. They were no longer operating in a unipolar world.

Two days later, he received an encrypted message from "Wang," a foreign asset he had cultivated in the Chinese diplomatic community—a young envoy posted to China's New York consulate. The man's cooperation had been the result of years of painstaking work. And the Chinese were skilled at pretending to be double agents. But this asset was legitimate, at least as far as John and his colleagues could tell.

"Party officials are getting ready to turn the screws," said Wang.

"More cyberattacks?" In recent weeks, China's cyberwarfare capabilities had knocked out local power grids, wreaked havoc with healthcare computer systems, and unleashed pervasive ransomware attacks against government, business, and educational targets.

"Probably. But I can't speak to that. I don't have that information. This is something else."

The agent then told him what he knew of the plan: the CCP was going to target another weak point: the medical supply. China would simply stop sending the medical products, devices, and raw materials the American people relied upon.

"Zero production. Zero export. Everything they make that you need—frozen. It's going to take a lot of manpower and bureaucracy to make it happen—to convey the order from the top to all the factories and logistics center—but basically, it's like flipping a switch," said Wang.

As an expert on China, John was aware of this vulnerability. He had written memos about it. But it always seemed, even to him, a backburner concern. For a country of a billion people, whose army boasted two million personnel and another half million reservists, plus a few hundred nukes at the ready, it hardly seemed like China needed to mess with aspirin to cause strife. But now, the ruthless simplicity of the plan was clear.

And then he thought of his daughter; the meds the oncologist had mentioned. Surely the stuff was made, or could be made, in America, right? But maybe not?

"That's the plan," Wang warned. "My advice? Start preparing now. You need their medical exports a lot more than they need your money."

Immediately, John dashed off a report summarizing his asset's allegations and offering his own prediction. The U.S. had about thirty days' worth of essential medical supplies in stock, not including medications that were already scarce because of the flu epidemic and supply chain issues that preceded the Taiwan crisis. There would be another thirty days' of supply in transit; primarily, in container ships east-bound in the Pacific. And then another thirty days of goods overseas either waiting for shipment or being produced—if, in fact, they even made it out of China, which seemed unlikely now.

Then John found his supervisor. This was information that had to be shared at the upper echelon—his boss's boss's boss. If true, this could change everything.

Pacific Ocean, July 10

In the Pacific, the tense standoff persisted as the U.S. and its allies controlled most of the seas east of Taiwan, but the blockade around the north, south, and west of Taiwan continued.

It was enough to grind most of Taiwan's maritime commerce to a standstill, but ships continued ferrying goods between China and Taiwan. That was a shrewd move: PRC President Shen did not want to starve the Taiwanese people into submission; he wanted to flex their might while demonstrating that the way of life the Taiwanese were accustomed to could continue—as long as they were willing to bend the knee to Beijing.

* * *

Captain Stavros Benos was furious.

His ship had been waiting for two days in China's Zhoushan port for the rest of its cargo to be loaded—seventeen shipping containers carrying protective gloves, masks, X-ray machines, pharmaceuticals, and other medical goods. He could not wait any longer.

No explanation—or rather, a handful of conflicting explanations—had been given for why the merchandise did not appear at port as scheduled. Normally, the workers in the port operated with ruthless efficiency.

Meanwhile, Sandro Miranda, the Filipino captain of another cargo vessel, the Totoralillo, was powering through the vast, aqueous expanse of the Pacific. While the ship flew the Panamanian flag, it was owned by COSCO Shipping, a subsidiary of the China Logistics Group, a shipping and transport behemoth that emerged in 2021 as a result of the merger of several state-owned enterprises. COSCO operated over a thousand container ships, and its parent company controlled dozens of railway lines, numerous warehouses and storage facilities, and over three million transport vehicles.100

On a sparkling, cloudless day, Captain Miranda received a curious communication: an order to turn around and head back to China. An order by whom? It wasn't specified. He suspected the Chinese authorities, who technically had no authority on these waters. But as a state-owned company, COSCO was under the thumb of the CCP. And the captain was not going to risk his job, his reputation, and perhaps even his freedom (who knew what repercussions awaited him if he defied the order?) by being insubordinate.

Hundreds of other ships crossing the vast body of water between Asia and the Americas at that moment, and under the control of China Logistics Groups, were also turned around. Back on the mainland, in the span of several days, Chinese factory owners all received a personal visit from Party officials accompanied by uniformed officers of the People's Liberation Army. All medical production destined for export was to be shut down. Any existing inventory was commandeered or ordered to be locked down. The trucks that normally showed up like clockwork every week to transport the goods from factory to port came as scheduled, but their drivers were turned away empty-handed.

And then, after a week, the trucks stopped coming too. Evidently, the trucking companies had gotten the message as well.

It presented a significant, but surmountable, logistical hurdle for the CCP to turn off the tap, which normally churned out manufacturing goods at high volume, seven days a week in a never-ending cycle of production, distribution, onloading, and shipping. But the Chinese state excels at top-down organization and coordination. Once the orders came down from on high, all it really took was dispatching designated bureaucrats or Party officials, along with uniformed soldiers as needed, to the factories, logistics centers, airports, and seaports to make sure the orders were communicated—and obeyed. There was little resistance. Why would there be?

* * *

In America, it didn't take long for the cascading effect to be felt by ordinary citizens.

The cargo vessels owned and operated by the China Logistics Group (and, by extension, the Chinese state) that ordinarily steamed in and out of ports up and down the West Coast disappeared. Of course, there were numerous other container ships belonging to private shipping companies of nations that did business in China, and the CCP could not order the owners of these vessels around. But they simply shut down the earlier part of the production process: those ships could enter Chinese ports, but there would be no medications or devices waiting to fill their containers.

So, in America, even when container ships arrived, there was nothing for the longshoremen and dockworkers to offload.

Nothing for the trucks that idled in the port to pick up.

Nothing to be delivered via truck to the wholesalers and distributors, which, in turn, had nothing to provide to the hospitals, healthcare facilities, clinics, drug stores, retail facilities, and individual patients—as they had for years, like clockwork.

This was like nothing anyone had seen before, not even during COVID. At that time, U.S.-bound maritime traffic out of China slowed dramatically, but goods still came through. This was a total shutdown.

Linney Pharmacy, Reston, Virginia, August 30

It was 5:30 a.m., thirty minutes before opening, and already the line outside was thirty deep. Harold Brown was one of those thirty, desperately hoping his acquaintanceship with Mr. Linney would get him a foot in the door, literally. Harold had run out of heparin weeks ago, which posed a grave threat to his health.

This was how Mr. Linney, the owner of the local pharmacy, operated now: waking up early, with the help of his staff, to serve as many customers he could, with what little remained in his inventory. First the cyberattacks had taken their toll, but he and his staff had managed. But there was nothing he could do about bare shelves. The problem went all the way up the supply chain.

He filled whatever prescriptions he could, but over the past two weeks, each day when the doors opened, most customers would be sent away empty-handed. It was a heartbreaking scene, with many people leaving in tears, terrified that the medicine they or their family members needed would be unobtainable anywhere.

Some customers just needed basic OTC stuff, but by then those shelves, too, were mostly bare. And it was hard to distinguish the price gougers and hoarders from people who genuinely needed product.

Despite all this, Mr. Linney was an indefatigable optimist.

He had survived a lot, both individually and as a citizen of a nation that had experienced periods of turmoil. He had lost his wife to cancer and his eldest son to suicide. He never lost hope.

This was no different. And yes, he read all the stories in the news about pharmacies that had been ransacked, looted, sometimes burned to the ground.

He didn't think it would happen to him.

He remained optimistic until the moment the first brick sailed through the plate glass window, shattering the vintage neon linney pharmacy sign that had hung there since the seventies.

You can't stop a determined mob, especially one driven by desperation. It's like a flood bursting through: they seep through every crack.

Suddenly, the usually orderly (if bitter) cluster of people waiting in line mutated into a seething mass of rage and frustration. They rampaged through the store, grabbing what they could.

"What are you doing? Don't you see you're stealing from each other, from neighbors who need the drugs the most?" Harold yelled. Mr. Linney also pleaded for them to calm down and disperse.

Such pleas did nothing to deter them. People leapt over the counter and rushed past the little swinging door leading to the pharmacy's stocks, snatching up pills, vials, boxes, everything. Did they even know what they were stealing?

Farouk was knocked to the ground by two men and a woman and overpowered. Someone struck Linney on the head from behind with a blunt object. His vision blurred and he crumpled to the ground.

They rushed over him, indifferent to the bleeding, unconscious pharmacist.

Outside, Harold dialed 911 on his cell phone, but the police had already fielded several calls. It was unlikely they would respond before the mob managed to pick over the store, and the Fairfax County PD weren't exactly trained for this scenario.

The 911 operator answered, but suddenly, Harold found that words escaped him. He tried to speak but it came out in a slurred mess. What was happening? Dizziness overtook him, and he felt an odd numbness on the left side of his body. With terror, he suddenly recognized what was unfolding: symptoms of stroke.

He collapsed, but no one seemed to notice. By the time the ambulance arrived, it was too late.

Kaiser Permanente, Reston, Virginia, September 10

Leah sat between her parents in the clinic waiting room. On the mounted TV, the news droned on about the crisis in Taiwan. John tried helplessly to tune it out. It would be nice to give his mind a rest from thinking about it. Constant preoccupation over the issue had compounded his grief over his father. In fact, he hadn't even really had time to mourn. But it was festering inside him. He felt like a drowning man struggling to keep his head above water.

His wife took notice and tried to distract him with idle chitchat about her brother, who was visiting them from out of town later that month.

The doctor strode into the waiting area, looking grim.

"I'm so sorry," he began, "someone was supposed to call you."

He smiled at Leah and said hello, then took her parents aside for a private chat.

"We cannot treat your daughter today. We do not have any more vincristine. Nowhere in our system. We've tried to go through every distributor. Please understand we're doing everything in our power to locate a supply. But, well, I'm sure you've seen the news . . ."

Carol exploded. "What do you mean? She has cancer! When will she be treated?"

"The nurse will schedule another appointment. Next week we have an opening. We're going to have to try another regimen."

"But you said vincristine was her best hope," Carol shot back.

"It is. And I won't mince words. The other drugs are not ideal. It's going to have to be a stopgap. Until we can get more supply."

"And that will be when?" asked Carol. But John knew the answer, which was that nobody knew. Or rather, until one of two superpowers could gain the upper hand. But it could take weeks, months, years. That was one thing they learned in the intelligence community: assess rationally, with the facts at your disposal, but make no assumptions, and expect the unexpected.

On the first floor, another, larger waiting room was overflowing with people. Two OR nurses were clad head to toe in black plastic trash bags.

White House, September 20

"People are dying, sir."

The president snapped a pencil in half in frustration. "You think I don't know that, goddamn it?" he shot back at his chief of staff.

"Politically, this is—"

"Politically, I don't need to tell you that this is bigger than politics," the president said.

"Yeah, that's uh, what I was going to say."

Present were the bigwigs of the republic, members of the major Cabinet positions, the speaker of the house, the VP, and the surgeon general. The White House was desperate to alleviate, if not solve, the public health disaster that China's withdrawal of exports had caused in just a couple months.

"We're the biggest economy in the world," President Rhodes said. "Still a manufacturing powerhouse. We put a man on the moon. We invented the internet. We made six different Rocky movies. We can beat China at their own game. They wanna freeze us out, we'll show them we don't need them at all."

"Nine, actually," said Mills.

"What?" Rhodes said.

"Nine Rocky films. If you count the Creeds."

The president shot him a look. "Mills," said Rhodes to the CIA director. "What can we expect next?"

"Actually, today, I've brought one of our analysts to handle the briefing. His knowledge of the Chinese military and political apparatus is unparalleled. Agent Brown?"

Normally, an invitation to brief the president would be a landmark achievement in a CIA analyst's career. But John felt no pleasure or pride in being there. That he was present was only a testament to how much the situation had devolved.

And if he was being honest with himself, he harbored some personal ill will toward the president, a man who by all accounts was doing the best he could with limited options but who was, however indirectly, responsible for the declining health of his little girl, not to mention the death of his father. The government should have foreseen China's weaponization of the medical supply. It had ample warning, including from John's own memos, which had evidently gone unheeded.

"Brown? Speak, please," the director said. John realized he was lost in thought, and had been staring hostilely at the president, who returned his gaze inscrutably.

John delivered an emotionless, clear-eyed assessment, but in fact there was little he said that wasn't already evident from the panic around the country. The Chinese plan to weaponize healthcare was working as intended, and the United States, John said, had no feasible recourse.

When he finished, Rhodes was dismissive of the analyst's sobering conclusions.

"If they want to fight a down-and-dirty trade war, we can give it right back to them," Rhodes said. "Electronics, agricultural products, automobiles, aviation—all the stuff we export to China. We'll cut off the tap and watch them squirm."

"Unfortunately, a tit-for-tat embargo of that kind is unlikely to be immediately effective, and might not even be impactful in the medium-term. Simply, we need their goods more than they need ours. Our exports to China have already been declining for several years. They can weather that storm."

The president turned to his secretary of state. "What about India? India is the world's medicine cabinet, is it not?"

The secretary of state cleared her throat. "The India strategy is a no-go."

"Meaning?"

"Meaning they don't want to antagonize China by taking sides. So they aren't going to ramp up production and exports for us."

"Who made this decision?"

"Mr. President, this is from the prime minister himself. We negotiated with him for hours. Morally and diplomatically, he's on our side. Practically speaking, they feel their hands are tied. China's got its hands around India too. All Beijing has to do is squeeze, and they holler. They told us the Chinese have threatened, in no uncertain terms, to cut off the raw materials from India's own pharma industry. So even if India wanted to play ball and help us out, it would only be a matter of time before China closed the tap for them too. And there's no other country even remotely capable of making the kinds of complex drugs we need, in the quantities we need them."

"Where the hell is Patterson?" yelled Rhodes. He had summoned the director of the Strategic National Stockpile—supposedly the bulwark against drug shortages: America's last hope.

"She's waiting outside," the chief of staff said.

But that was just another bracing splash of cold water. The SNS director calmly but firmly informed the president that the SNS's own resources had been strained. The SNS was a stopgap for the commercial market, not a replacement. And, Patterson reminded, since COVID, when the pandemic exposed the inadequacies of the system, she had been clamoring for more funding and more resources, had testified on the Hill twice, had done all she could to shore up the stockpile. But like most things in Congress, the issue received some half-hearted attention before being buried in the avalanche of whatever minutiae they were working on (or not working on, the president added joylessly).

Later that day, another conference call with the Pharmaceutical Research and Manufacturers of America (PhRMA) and several drug company executives was similarly fruitless. President Rhodes was ready to muster all his political capital to persuade—or even force, to the extent legally possible—factories in America to produce what was needed.

But the truth was that it wasn't a question of political or economic will. Not even Big Pharma could remedy the scarcity. First, even by ramping up production, the list of drugs made in America, with raw materials sourced domestically or from friendly nations, was short. So even if by some miracle they could construct a dozen new factories overnight, the assembly line would not be running without the raw materials for drugs imported from China.

15. Brown residence, Reston, Virginia, September 29

John sat on his daughter's bed, mopping her brow with a washrag. She had been in a state of feverish sleep for the whole day, unable to eat, barely able to keep down a few sips of water. Her body was fighting not just the cancer but a secondary infection.

Even through the course of this terrible disease, his spirited little girl had maintained her spark. Now, she was virtually comatose.

"She's getting worse," said Carol, standing in the doorway of the bedroom. "She needs the medicine, John!"

John fought off tears. She was right.

Carol wept profusely. "First your father. Who's next, our little girl? How much longer? How many people have to die before this is over?"

* * *

Meanwhile, in the White House, President Rhodes resisted his advisers' urging to make a prime-time statement about the crisis surrounding the deteriorating medical supply system. The CCP's strategy had never been officially announced and the federal government did not officially recognize it as a crisis. Doing so, Rhodes reasoned, would only add fuel to the fire. The Chinese couldn't know how devastating their tactic was. But it was naïve to think they weren't aware. What had started slowly and insidiously—localized scarcity here and there—had grown into a full-blown, systemic catastrophe. By the time the U.S. realized what was happening, it was too late.

A black market for medical supplies, everything from aspirin to rare and complex prescription pills, had grown up overnight, fueled by the dark web and regular old street dealers. But doing business with black marketeers carried its own risks, and already, hundreds of Americans had been hospitalized or killed from consuming tainted or counterfeit medicines of unknown provenance. There was speculation, on conspiracy-minded message boards as well as in the intel community, that operatives in China had deliberately poisoned a drug shipment bound for the U.S., a diabolically shrewd tactic. There was no proof. But the fear these incidents provoked was enough to throw more fuel on the fire.

Scarcity of antibiotics like tetracycline and doxycycline had caused infectious disease to spread like wildfire and many patients who would have otherwise survived became gravely ill or perished. Fresh outbreaks of a new bacterial disease emerged in the Pacific Northwest. But hospitals quickly ran out of vancomycin, a last-resort antibiotic made domestically but with APIs from China.

People with high blood pressure couldn't get their valsaratan. Even ibuprofen and hydrocortisone became prized products, hard to get, coveted zealously by those who needed them.

Malfunctioning imaging technology (MRI machines, CAT scanners, etc.), digital diagnostic equipment, patient monitors, and other essential tech could not be repaired or replaced. Spare parts quickly ran out. And the little domestic production that existed ground to a halt when microchip exports from Taiwan plummeted.

Larger healthcare organizations had mustered a spotty defense against the relentless cyberattacks, but Beijing was constantly unleashing new forms of malware to cripple hospital computer systems. Even something as simple as record-keeping became unreliable—and the consequences when doctors couldn't access a patient's medical history became fatal. Physicians and nurses tried to adapt and "go analog," but they found that for many functions, it was impossible. The tech had simply advanced too far. There was no nontechnological fallback.

And all this had a compounding effect on the already raging epidemic, since the more the healthcare system was impaired, the more treatment became inaccessible and the more rapidly the disease spread.

It wasn't just tragic, it was embarrassing. The U.S. looked like a failed state.

Pressure on the White House mounted. The American people needed leadership and they weren't buying that the government of the most powerful country in the world was powerless. But it was true. If planning had started years ago, this crisis could have been averted. The mighty dragon had struck, and it struck in the place America was weakest.

At the next Oval Office meeting, the secretary of state, leaders of the intelligence community, and the DoD and joint chiefs of staff reiterated their stark choice. Clearly, the nation could not go on like this. They had to get China to release its stranglehold on the medical supply. There were only two options: engage China in warfare and muster enough force to compel them to get the factories running and the ships sailing again, or withdraw its Pacific forces and leave Taiwan to the wolves. That would also mean giving the PRC control of Taiwan's economically vital and strategically valuable semiconductor industry—more than half of the world's microchips were made there.

A war with China was unthinkable. It would be devastating, bloody, protracted, and unpredictable—nuclear powers had never before fought head to head. Not to mention, in all likelihood, politically untenable. Americans cared a lot more about getting their medicine than keeping a distant island nation free.

The president, looking ashen and grim, cleared his throat. "Get Beijing on the line."

16. Taipei, Taiwan, one week later

After the U.S. had brokered a deal with China to resume exports of medicine, medical devices, raw materials, protective gear, and everything else the healthcare system depended on to function, Taiwan faced the grim prospect of facing China alone. Without U.S. commitment, Japan, Europe, and other allies were unwilling to commit troops or naval forces, much less get involved in an air or ground war on the Chinese mainland. Taiwan's military was formidable, and a successful Chinese conquest was by no means a foregone conclusion, but at the eleventh hour, the authorities in Taiwan chose peaceful surrender rather than a war that would have devastated the island and killed tens of thousands, if not more. It was a choice backed by most of the Taiwanese people, who, seeing that they were isolated, recognized that war with China would have been suicidal. And it might not even preserve their independence in the end.

Chih-weh and his parents watched the unbelievable scene from their apartment window. Chinese battle tanks bearing the red star of the People's Republic rolled down the highway, accompanied by a legion of troop transport trucks, APVs, and other military vehicles, a seemingly unending parade of invaders. They had arrived. And who knew when, if ever, they would leave.

CHAPTER 9

WHAT MUST BE DONE: SOLUTIONS

At present, there is very little movement, either in the halls of Washington, the C-suites of healthcare companies, or the blue-collared, hardworking communities across America to change the status quo. Many people who have skin in the game, both on the business side and the medical side, recognize the extent of the problem, but it is the kind of problem that can only be redressed by a broad-based coalition of public and private actors, whose collective power can achieve the policy solutions and practical implementation that will spur a new age of American innovation and independence.

As David Sanders told me, "We have a silent Cold War happening in the medical product arena between China and the West. We need to recognize it, own up to it, and do something to boost our domestic and allied production." The solution, in short, is to wean ourselves off our dependency on nations that do not have our best interest at heart, lest that cold war become a hot one.

The following initiatives can achieve this.

1. *Institute a federal policy of transparency that mandates the availability of all data regarding the manufacturing and tracking of the medical supply chain, including sourcing, quality, volume, and capacity.*

As the oft-quoted business mantra says, what gets measured gets done.

You can't fix a problem until you can accurately assess it. Currently it is impossible to report on our status with respect to what supplies are available where, which items are at risk of shortage, where the supply chain is most likely to break down, and where it is more secure.

We are stymied by many unanswered questions, such as exactly how much of our medical supply is of foreign origin? Which products are made in China or other hostile nations? Even after all the Operation Warp Speed drama, no one—not even us—could tell you precisely how many needles and syringes are manufactured annually in the United States, how that production is distributed, and how much remains in reserve. We know the 'big stuff' but there's not a database where you can look at every single product, understand its supply chain, point of origin, volume of production, and use. How can we formulate an effective healthcare security policy without knowing how much—or how little—of vital, life-sustaining resources are in store? We need a database that tells us where the supply chain is robust and where it is likely to break down. It could be maintained by the FDA, which has the expertise and wherewithal for this kind of information tracking. Companies might balk at being asked to disclose such information, which they might guard as a "trade secret," but it will be regulatory law: such is the cost of doing business.

Concomitant to the objective of transparency is *better labeling on medical products*. No more obfuscation and ambiguity: the end user should have accurate information about where something is made, and not just its final point of assembly but the geographic provenance of its constituent parts.

Presently, it is too easy to obscure the origin of a pill or device. Gibson and Singh note in *China Rx* that "Country-of-origin labeling requirements for prescription drugs are so confusing that even veterans in the industry are confused about where their medicines are made. . . . The FDA has its own rules that make it easier for companies to hide the country of origin. Once a drug is in the United States, the label has to include the name and place of the business of the manufacturer, packer, or distributor."[101] But the "place of business" can be distinct from country of origin. It's a loophole that conceals the truth from patients and doctors.

Producers should identify, both in a public database and, to the extent it is feasible, on the product packaging itself, the manufacturing site, the FDA Establishment Identifier (FEI), the city, and the country. API manufacturers must be mandated to disclose the sources of raw materials.

2. *Implement a national strategy of reshoring.*

Reshoring is the watchword of the future: turn back the clock on decades-long offshoring and bring medical production back home. No, we're not going to resurrect a 1950s-style era of American manufacturing dominance, nor can we rely completely on domestic sources for the supply chain. But we can restore the balance.

Reshoring will require federal intervention to incentivize private industry to make the necessary investment and neutralize, in part, the economic advantages of operating factories in China, India, and elsewhere. Without some form of federal support, it will be impossible for suppliers to compete and for patients/consumers to afford costlier, domestically produced products.

Reshoring can be accomplished with a combination of "push and pull" incentives.

"Push" gets product out the door. It's a direct investment that ensures profitability. These take the form of upfront grants, R&D tax credits, smart deregulatory measures (while being careful to avoid a "race to the bottom" with China on environmental and labor protections), etc. It might involve some subsidies for individual purchasers of pharmaceuticals or devices so that American citizens are not forced to absorb the pain of higher prices (though to be fair, it is not a foregone conclusion that reshoring will mean higher prices for consumers.)

"Pull" incentives are more nebulous and rely on "pulling" companies back by providing confidence in future profits and long-term viability. These are nuanced conversations like reimbursement reform and long-term contracting and procurement opportunities.

A legislative model for encouraging reshoring could be something like the 2022 CHIPS and Science Act, which provides billions of dollars in R&D and subsidies for the semiconductor industry in order to boost domestic microchip production, which, as discussed, is perilously concentrated in East Asia. If Congress recognizes the national security importance of semiconductors, surely it can do the same for our healthcare system.

Of course, there would be strings attached to any federal aid to private industry. There would be milestones that any recipient of federal grant, loan, or tax break dollars must adhere to. The money would come in segments and in the event of a missed milestone, the faucet turns off. Other conditions could be legally imposed; for example, recipient companies would be forbidden from stock buybacks for a certain period of time—similar to what some senators have urged for the semiconductor industry in light of the CHIPS Act.[102]

3. *Utilize the United States' full domestic industrial capacity through revamping.*

It's not just about reshoring, but about *revamping*: leveraging existing excess productive capacity in the United States. Thirty percent of the pharmaceutical manufacturing sites in the United States are at or less than 50 percent utilization.[103] Only about 5 percent are at full capacity. So the industry *could* be churning out locally made drugs at a much higher volume.

The reason for underutilization is also the solution: lack of commitment from the government as a buyer. There is a mismatch of utilization and demand. The commercial market and the government market for certain pharmaceuticals are wildly different. The federal government is the number-one purchaser of prescription drugs, either directly or via subsidized health insurance programs.

Many drugs, medical supplies, and devices are not produced for the commercial market, and even for popular drugs, such as Tamiflu, the government is often the primary purchaser.

Therefore, many American factories respond to singular spikes in demand for particular drugs that are not commercially popular, and the rest of the time go through periods of underutilization. We can take advantage of these "in between" periods to manufacture the perennially in-demand drugs that we are now producing in India and China.

We don't need to build a host of new factories to bridge the manufacturing gap. The factories are extant, operable, and FDA-approved. If the government commits to buying domestically made pharmaceuticals, the industry is capable of meeting that demand.

4. *The federal government must take the lead in creating a true public-private partnership.*

A complex, multifaceted problem demands complex, multifaceted solutions involving a coalition of stakeholders in the government, medical, and business communities. The federal government must lead the charge and broker collaboration between these disparate groups.

There's a little-known administration at the Department of Health and Human Services called the Administration for Strategic Preparedness and Response (ASPR) that handles, as the name implies, preparing for and responding to public health emergencies. Within it, there is an entity called the Biomedical Advanced Research and Development Authority (BARDA), whose core mission is to assist the private sector with the advanced research and development efforts of critical medical countermeasures.

BARDA has worked with over sixty-four products that received FDA approvals, licensures, and clearances. During the pandemic, it supported 164 COVID-19 partnerships, including 102 biomedical products supported for the COVID-19 response. ASPR and BARDA have the mandate, expertise, personnel, and organizational heft to spearhead a public-private partnership.

One of BARDA's most promising initiatives is called Industrial-Based Expansion, or IBx. Through IBx, the government partners with private industry "to increase the domestic industrial base to allow for the additional raw material and consumables production necessary to support the manufacturing of therapeutics and vaccines during a public health emergency or pandemic," including ancillary supplies (needles, syringes, vials, etc.).[104] BARDA also funds "next generation" R&D to encourage innovation. It's a relatively new program and still finding its feet, but it's an encouraging example of what can be achieved when private industry and government health departments join forces.

5. *Private industry must form its own "coalition within a coalition" to promote a stronger, domestic-centered supply chain.*

Several groups, most notably the Securing America's Medicines and Supply (SAMS) Coalition, have been created over the past three years to address the gap between private industry innovation and the power of the federal government, exchange ideas, and advocate for smart solutions to a problem that afflicts all Americans. Such associations can exist in parallel with the private-public coalitions we've already talked about. Companies in the medical supply business can better advance their common aim of domesticating production if they collaborate formally.

The SAMS Coalition, for example, of which iRemedy is a member, lobbies for reforms to trade and tax law to stimulate domestic production, coordinates with the National Institutes of Health and BARDA to expand loan, grant, and purchase agreement programs related to the medical supply, and advocates for shoring up the Strategic National Stockpile. Collectively, we are able to advocate for policy change, endorse certain bills, propose amendments, push for action on Capitol Hill, and create noise around the topic. When these groups are comprised of industry leaders, the government listens.

6. *Leverage the purchasing power of the federal government and large national healthcare systems to encourage domestic production.*

The federal government provides healthcare to millions of people though Medicare (around sixty-one million patients) and the Veterans Administration (VA) (around nine million patients). The DoD and other federal entities also routinely purchase medical gear, drugs, and devices. This is a tremendous source of influence because when you're the one writing the checks, you call the shots. The government can strategically direct its capital to where it provides the greatest benefit, with appropriate legal structures and compliance requirements in place to ensure that such programs are not just a giveaway to the drug industry, and that the benefits are directed to the public at large.

Medicare is especially powerful because it basically sets the bar for the whole industry, private insurers included. Where Medicare goes, others follow. Medicare is not a healthcare provider per se; it's more like an insurance company in that it reimburses health providers for services, drugs, and devices. Therefore, it can use that position to incentivize "Made in America" initiatives; for example, by reimbursing at a higher rate healthcare providers who prescribe domestically produced drugs versus foreign-made alternatives.

For-profit healthcare providers and insurance companies are constantly looking to cut costs and boost profits. If they can pay less for a foreign-made product, they're going to do so. That's the whole problem. Medicare can mitigate this by changing the economics of the whole game and ensuring the incentives align with the goal.

Recently, Medicare upped "payment adjustments" to healthcare organizations buying American-made N95 respirators, recognizing that although those respirators are more expensive, it is worth the expense. By putting their money where their mouth is, Medicare is demonstrating a commitment to eliminating foreign dependence.

The U.S. healthcare market is dominated by large healthcare systems comprised of hospitals, surgery centers, physician offices, imaging centers, labs and pharmacies. These systems may be for-profit, nonprofit, community or faith-based, and many spend billions of dollars in medical supplies and are dependent on a reliable supply chain. These large healthcare provider organizations must make their own commitment to American-made products and view doing so as part of a long-term strategy to secure supply and stabilize costs.

A commitment must also be made to support the "small businesses" that build these domestic manufacturing facilities. After all, the U.S. economy has historically thrived largely because of the innovation and capital risk invested by our entrepreneurs and venture capitalists. While the government sets aside a share of its procurement contracts for small businesses, this commitment is often not met in the real world.

I've already witnessed firsthand dozens of small businesses working to build domestic factories, often with confusing or nonexistent support from the U.S. government. iRemedy's own experience through our participation in Operation Warp Speed demonstrates how contract changes by the government can expose small businesses, such as mine, to massive losses.

7. *Forge a multilateral agreement between nations that prohibits export bans and restrictions on key medical supply products during global health emergencies.*

"Every man for himself" is a poor strategy for combatting a worldwide problem, as we have seen during the pandemic. Cooperation, collaboration, and resource sharing between nations is a better path out of a mass health crisis. Consequently, countries should be legally bound not to restrict exports of key supplies. A single broken link in the supply chain causes chaos for everyone.

This agreement could be negotiated under the authority of the World Trade Organization or perhaps the United Nations. Signatory nations that violate the agreement would be subject to reputational, legal, or economic penalties.

No country is truly self-sufficient when it comes to the medical supply chain, and this fact in and of itself should incentivize a spirit of cooperation: what goes around comes around, and if one country withholds its vital supplies, it could spur a retaliatory export ban by another nation, even a friendly one. Better if we all collectively agree to keep the gears of production and export moving, even during a crisis.

8. *Rely more on our allies and their role in the medical supply chain.*

When I talk about "Made in America," I don't mean in an absolute sense. Some products, including their raw materials, can be 100 percent produced stateside. But many things *will* require the involvement of other economies. That is just the reality of globalization, which, even if we are (as some have predicted) on the cusp of an era of "deglobalization," will remain the dominant paradigm of commercial production in all industries.

So a looser definition of "Made in America" involves making what we can at home while relying on our allies, rather than China or some other hostile state, for component parts, raw materials, or labor we cannot muster at home. As David Sanders told me, "If you can build facilities in Mexico, Poland, or Israel, that's much better than relying on a country that could shut off all exportation in the future."

This will have the added effect of shoring up longstanding diplomatic and economic partnerships with the nations that we have come to count on for decades.

9. *Replenish the Strategic National Stockpile and overhaul the means by which inventory is tracked and dispensed.*

The SNS was conceived to handle localized, temporary medical emergencies, such as a natural disaster or a bioterror attack. It was not designed as a fallback during a sustained, nationwide health crisis such as a pandemic. Now we know that we must be ready for the latter as well as the former.

Consequently, the size and scope of SNS inventory must grow dramatically. But it isn't just a matter of keeping the shelves stocked. We need more transparency about the SNS in terms of what is available, how much is allocated to which state, and how to access it. When the coronavirus struck, state and local public health officials were in the dark about where the SNS stockpiles physically were or how to procure products their citizens needed. Better management and greater integration between the SNS and other federal agencies, as well as state and local governments, will help remedy this. We need a national approach, coordinated with local governments, that can assure adequate supply for 350 million Americans.

Yes, that will be costly and complicated, requiring warehousing of immense quantities of supplies. But I think we can all agree that none of us would ever like to again see ER nurses wearing trash bags, or read about doctors being forced to make impossible triage decisions about which ailing patients get hooked up to a ventilator and which have to die because there aren't enough to go around.

Better inventory management can offset the burden of warehousing all this stuff. Medical supplies don't last forever; generally they're good for about five years before you need to dispose of them, which is both a waste of money and has an adverse environmental impact.

However, if we rotate SNS supplies back into the private market while they still have a shelf life, then we'll avoid a situation where we're storing vast quantities of materials just to burn or dump them later on. This is logistically tricky but by no means unfeasible; it's just a matter, like everything else, of mustering the will and the resources.

10. *Identify upstream supply chain shortages before they snowball into major bottlenecks.*

The SAMS Coalition is vigilant about this, as is iRemedy; as I mentioned, one of our unique value propositions is forecasting scarcity and plugging the gaps before anyone else. A disruption in manufacturing of vital goods often originates far from the assembly line, in a field or quarry or mine or lab where the raw materials for the final product are harvested. By tracking the raw materials more closely, we can stop a problem before it starts.

Certain drugs are at greater risk of scarcity than others, and we should identify these. Hospitals, which are often blindsided by shortages, should be looped into networks and databases that track such things. Forecasting should be done on both a short-term and long-term basis so we have a more comprehensive view of what will be needed when.

Finally, we should prioritize tracking medicines whose supply disruption would cause immediate and widespread harm to the public.

11. Improve the FDA's overseas inspections capability

This is a short-term rather than a long-term remedy since, of course, the overarching goal is to shift production *away* from foreign powers. Doing so would obviate the need for FDA inspectors to journey across the sea and deep into the mainland of China just to make sure the aspirin or amoxicillin you're taking at breakfast isn't fabricated in a dirty factory with no safeguards.

Until then, foreign FDA inspections are a stopgap measure, and one that could be drastically improved. We should make FDA inspections swifter and more comprehensive. If that means Congress needs to expand the agency's budget to hire more people and pay for their visits, it is certainly worth the cost. But "virtual inspections," which have yet to be implemented, provide a cost-effective method that obliterates the limitations of time and space. If health-related lockdowns prevent agents from traveling, then virtual inspections will be the *only* recourse.

12. Rethink and retool our relationship with China.

It is time to renegotiate the terms of the Sino-American economic partnership. Shifting the locus of the supply chain to the U.S. and our allies closer to home will take, at best, fifteen to twenty years, and a complete disengagement from China is virtually inconceivable (absent of war, which will benefit nobody.) It will be more like a divorce that ends a marriage of convenience; you leave each other's orbit, but you still need to maintain relations for the sake of the kids.

This divorce from China is going to be long, messy, and probably acrimonious, but it doesn't mean it has to be destructive, nor that we have to cede our power at the bargaining table. (As a recent analogue, one might consider the West cutting business ties with Russia, basically overnight, following its invasion of Ukraine. That includes European nations that were heavily dependent on Russian energy.) It may not be easy but if the situation demands it, you find a way.

The U.S. *does* possess leverage in its relationship with Beijing. For a long time we have let Beijing call the shots, but we are still the world's sole superpower. In many respects, China is as dependent on us as we are on them. Trade is a two-way street; while we rely on them for imported goods, they need access to our markets for their exports. China also needs foreign inputs to fuel its manufacturing, and the U.S. is the primary source of foreign input for its industry.[105] China wants access to our technology and hopes that U.S. blue chip firms set up shop there. Tens of thousands of Chinese citizens work, live, and study in the U.S., and the Chinese middle class is a big consumer of American media, a form of soft power. The Trans-Pacific Partnership and the Indo-Pacific Economic Framework for Prosperity, both led by the U.S., present a multilateral economic counterweight to China's efforts to bring other Asian and Pacific states within its sphere of influence. China seeks an increasingly bigger share of global prestige, and the U.S., as superpower and unofficial leader of the free world, remains a gatekeeper at the entrance to the club.

These are all bargaining chips that can be used to carve out a better China policy that corrects some of the disequilibrium that underlies our current relationship and obviates the risk of conflict escalation or even war, which in the long run would be disastrous for both parties and likely the entire world. Time is of the essence. We still hold the cards. Let's not wait until China is too powerful to respond to any form of U.S. pressure.

A Look at Current (and Future) Legislation: Is It Adequate?

With its vast size and multitrillion-dollar budget, the federal government can and should throw its weight around, providing subsidies and tax breaks for private industry to keep the factories stateside, making it more viable for health insurers and healthcare organizations reimbursed or funded by the government to buy American supplies. The federal government can also shape patterns of consumption and production by awarding lucrative federal contracts to companies that comply with certain criteria, as it does currently.

Limits on federal government power and funding are essential to our democratic republic. These limits are enshrined in our Constitution, along with personal property, privacy, freedom of speech, and other liberties that create American exceptionalism, making us a great nation. But securing our medical supply chain, to protect the lives of our citizens, is an appropriate national defense mandate that cannot be ignored.

The executive branch already has a broad mandate, and funding, to make a difference. But since Congress holds the power of the purse, new legislation is needed to break the cycle of foreign dependence and realize a long-term "Made in America" strategy.

There are a few helpful laws on the books already, along with others that, as of this writing, are being discussed on Capitol Hill.

1. Trade Agreements Act (TAA): This 1979 law was designed to encourage free trade. It stipulates that government agencies can only purchase U.S.-made goods or goods produced in a list of around a hundred approved countries. China, India, Indonesia, Iran, Iraq, Malaysia, Pakistan, and Russia are specifically *not* TAA-approved.

   One problem with the TAA is that it's too easy to legally evade the system. If you can demonstrate that none of the "approved" countries, or the U.S., can supply what you need, then you can be granted a waiver to use China, India, or one of the other "banned" countries. These waivers are given out as easily as the free samples at Costco.

2. Barry Amendment: The Barry Amendment requires that the DoD give preference in procurement to products made wholly in the U.S., including raw materials. It's one of the stricter "Made in America" regulations on the books, and it's why the DoD originally wanted all the needles made in the U.S. As you can see by our example, however, when this isn't possible, we're forced to look elsewhere.

3. Transparency in Drug Labeling Act: This bill was a promising impetus for reform when it was introduced in 2008, but it was killed in committee before it gained traction. According to *China Rx* authors Gibson and Singh, citing an "industry insider," the bill was torpedoed by lobbyists working for Big Pharma, which neither wanted the extra burden of labeling nor to shed light on the uncomfortable truth about drug sourcing.[106]

4. American Made Medicine Act: Introduced in 2022 but not yet in committee, this bill seeks to strengthen the domestic medical supply chain through a combination of tax reductions and investment tax credits that incentivize industry and investment.

    That program is not to be confused with the:

5. American Made Pharmaceuticals Act: Also introduced in 2022, this bipartisan bill, currently in committee, would provide preferential treatment for U.S.-made drugs funded by Medicare, Medicaid, and CHIP; mandate greater transparency by pharma companies about where drugs are made; and add other incentives to plug the gaps in the supply chain.

6. PREVENT Pandemics Act: PREVENT is an acronym meaning "Prepare for and Respond to Existing Viruses, Emerging New Threats." This 2022 Senate bill, which is publicly backed by about a hundred healthcare organizations and

universities,[107] would generally improve key areas of public health and also address the medical supply question. It has not advanced passed the introduction stage.

7. Bipartisan Infrastructure Law: A rare piece of landmark legislation passed by Congress in an era of partisan gridlock, the BIL is not specific to healthcare. But some of its provisions assist the development of the medical supply chain directly as well as indirectly, as subsidizing infrastructure is a boon for industry generally (and why China is betting so heavily on its transcontinental Belt and Road Initiative as well as domestic infrastructure projects.)

What Price Health?

One of the biggest objections to recentering the supply chain in the U.S. and its allies is cold, hard economics. You just can't beat China and India on production costs. Labor, raw materials, assembly, currency manipulation: it's just cheaper. Companies don't want to sacrifice the bottom line and consumers and patients don't want to pay extra. It would be nice if it were economically feasible to reshore, but it's not, say skeptics.

There are three flaws with this argument.

First, while yes, China does offer a competitive advantage in this respect, that advantage is not as pronounced as it once was. Other countries with a strong manufacturing base, such as Vietnam and, closer to home, Mexico, offer similar bang for the buck. And let's not forget that anything made in China for export incurs transport costs. Moving stuff across the largest ocean in the world is not inexpensive.

Furthermore, we can offset paying more for domestic production with prudent federal intervention (subsidies, tax breaks, low-interest loans, reimbursements, grants to consumers.)

The objection to that approach might be that we're just robbing Peter to pay Paul; that such measures will add to an already bloated federal budget, that it's a form of corporate welfare, or that the government shouldn't stick its fingers in private enterprise or pick and choose which industries get preferential treatment.

But that leads me to my second point, which is that using taxpayer funds to encourage reshoring should be seen less as an *expense* and more as an *investment* in our collective health and security. The "cheapness" of foreign-made medical supplies conceals the high cost of risk. When production is located oceans away, and under the authority of a hostile power, the normally reliable flow of vital medicines and life-sustaining devices can be cut off instantly. The resulting scarcity, in the absence of an alternative source, would send prices skyward, cause healthcare costs to surge as patients who can no longer get what they need for day-to-day health maintenance end up hospitalized, and, if the shortages are long and severe enough, lead to incalculable human suffering. No amount of short-term savings can justify this.

Third, the economic boon that results from growing our domestic manufacturing base will also help mitigate higher "Made in America" production costs and additional federal spending. This is a secondary argument—we need to reassert control over the medical supply chain regardless of whether it's economically advantageous or not, since it's a matter of public health and national security. But it *is* a nonnegligible benefit, especially when there is so much talk of "bringing American jobs back home" and "resurrecting American industry." Why not make medical supplies the vanguard of that campaign? Cut the ribbon on new factories, train the next generation of skilled workers and innovators, create jobs, generate wealth, and keep more of our money at home instead of sending it abroad to line the coffers of the Chinese Communist Party?

We will never be completely self-reliant, but we will have won when the majority of our medical supplies production is concentrated either in the United States or in allied nations (preferably those allies close to our own borders.) The solutions will not be easy to implement, but they are doable. What we need is *commitment.* It cannot happen with half-hearted gestures or inconsistent, tenuous efforts. All stakeholders (federal and state governments, public health agencies, medical professionals, healthcare providers, private companies operating in the medical supply space, patient organizations, and the public at large) need to be on board, fully engaged, with the federal government leading the way. That means not doing things like abruptly and unilaterally changing the terms of a contract when your contractor has already put their company on the line to fulfill it, as happened to us in the middle of the pandemic. I know that small factories were put together during COVID to make masks or gowns, on the belief that the government was going to act as a buyer, but due to the on-again off-again nature of the government funding process, those contracts never came through. And the factories suffered as a result. Private industry and healthcare organizations are accustomed to the status quo and are only going to make the necessary changes if they know the government has their back.

It will be a challenge, no doubt. Any major, multiyear, broad-based program is—especially in a pluralist democracy like ours, where innumerable special interest groups work at cross-purposes, the membership of our national legislature is a constant churn, and a new chief executive enters office every four to eight years. Our decentralized, federalist system also engenders a patchwork, piecemeal approach: a little here, a little there, while the nature of the problem demands coordinated and consistent action.

But in spite of the challenges, achieving this is in *everyone's* interest. That we can take for granted. And that alone should be enough to break through the gridlock and mobilize everyone into action.

EPILOGUE

By spring 2021, the worst of the pandemic had passed, both for the nation as a whole and for our company's mission as part of Operation Warp Speed. Illness was on the ebb. Locked-down cities and states were opening. And Americans were lining up by the millions to get their shot in the arm. In April 2021, we were delivering fifty million needle/syringe combinations every week, via several aircraft *per day*, thanks in part to Crane's effective handling of the logistics. Crane was flying the needles into U.S. airports as well as Canadian ones (using converted Air Canada passenger jets along with cargo jets), then trucking them over our northern border. Whatever it took to keep health facilities supplied.

Then, in June 2021, one of our factories alerted us to a defect in one of the batches they'd sent out—over two million items that we had already delivered to the government were faulty. That is to be expected in high-volume manufacturing, but obviously it's still an urgent cause for concern. Thankfully, that batch hadn't yet left the government's facility. We were able to trace, collect, destroy and replace 2,358,200 needles and syringes, at no cost to the government. Our vigilance and quick action put us in good graces with the government, which despite the rocky beginning could see that we had come through on our promises.

By August 2021, when 85 percent of the total contract had been fulfilled, we received some unexpected attention when Republican Congressman Brian Mast of Florida's

21st District appeared at iRemedy's office in Stuart with a TV news crew. He was excited a small local company had played such an essential role in vaccinating the public and wanted to tout the story.

That same month, we got a surprising email from the chairman of our primary factory (who communicated via his English-speaking daughter, who is VP of business development there). Until this moment, we'd had no direct contact with the factories. The intermediaries handled that. But purely by accident, the chairman found my email address buried in an email chain between iRemedy, the factory, and the various middlemen we had no choice but to work with. The brokers had gone to great lengths to prevent any direct communication between the factory and us, lest they be cut out.

Finally, we had a chance to speak, man to man, albeit digitally. And he was shocked to hear how we had basically been blackmailed into forking over millions upon millions in deposits. I was surprised at *his* surprise. Evidently, the brokers had been doing what unscrupulous brokers do best: playing both ends against the middle. The chairman and I expressed frustration with these middlemen and complained how they weren't treating us, or him, fairly, how they were basically leeches who added no real value but profited handsomely. The damage had been done, but it was reassuring to know there were still people with integrity.

During this period, we were still constantly battling intermediaries over payments and withheld deposits, and it was a struggle to even ascertain who *had* our deposits. We had bet the farm on this operation and the lack of clear answers regarding custody was harrowing. Besides the usual time zone disparities and language gaps (which were no less frustrating now than at the start of the pandemic), when you do business in China, it is hard to tell who is who. As mentioned, Chinese who deal with Westerners usually give themselves Western names, so you find yourself in a confusing email thread or WhatsApp conversation with three different guys named James, all of whom are trying to pass the buck to the other Jameses.

Nevertheless, as spring turned to summer turned to fall, the wheels kept turning: needles came flying off the assembly line by the millions, to be boxed up, loaded on pallets, trucked to the airport, flown to Chicago or Toronto, and distributed to government warehouses, after which they were dispatched to medical facilities and vaccination sites. We completed the last delivery to the government on November 1, 2021, almost one year to the day after the first delivery. In total, over one billion items (541,000,000 needles and 541,000,000 syringes) were produced, shipped, and delivered, requiring 2,055 trucks (5.5 trucks per day) and 150 aircrafts to deliver 796,052 cartons. We manufactured 10,677 miles of medical grade steel, just from the 1"-1.5" needle tip—nearly enough to reach from Los Angeles to Beijing and back again.

One afternoon about a week later, a FedEx deliverywoman rang my bell. I wasn't expecting anything, and hoped, only half-jokingly, it wasn't some destructive item—a fistful of anthrax, an explosive device. Or, worse, an invoice demanding another seven-figure deposit from one of the many adversaries—foiled con artists, unhappy contractors, Uzbekistani Airlines pilots, and hostile operatives in the Chinese government—we had inadvertently made over the last year and a half. Unlikely, but one wonders.

I tentatively opened the box and tore away the packaging. There was Phil's hand-crafted knife, the one he had promised me over a year ago, when everything was falling apart and so many people were doubting our ability to execute this impossible, gargantuan contract.

The curved, scimitar-like blade, about eight inches long, attached to a smooth cherrywood handle, and polished to a gleam, came to a sharp point, like a punctuation mark at the end of a sentence, as if to say *We did it.*

Phil had mounted it on a wooden plaque with this inscription:

Operation Warp Speed
iRemedy Healthcare & Goldbelt Security
1,082,000,000 needles and syringes.

I gingerly touched the blade to gauge its sharpness. That dagger was no toy or mere ceremonial object. It was the real deal, made with care and expertise, and sharp enough to cut through a thousand miles of red tape. It was a fitting symbol and a reminder that shipping those needles and syringes wasn't just business. It had been knock-down, drag-out, hand-to-hand combat, on a battlefield that encompassed the whole world. Worse, between Northfield, Goldbelt, the Department of Defense, the brokers, the factories and Chinese Communist Party, it was impossible to tell friend from foe.

Ironically, the biggest contract in our company's history has been, for us, a financial disaster. Not only did we not turn a profit, but we ended up in the red. We hold no ill will toward the folks at the DoD, but because the government changed the required specification of the type of needle from conventional to safety, iRemedy had to stash all the unwanted needles (for which we did not get paid) somewhere. Today, we are storing two hundred million needles and syringes (enough to fill ten Costcos) in warehouses in China, Malaysia, and the U.S. Every day we battle Chinese brokers who are fraudulently trying to seize our inventory, and we're still fighting to get millions of dollars in deposits back. Little by little, we're finding buyers for the surplus, but it remains a thorn in the side of our small company. We've been told by our logistics partner, which has staff in China, that these same brokers are agents of the CCP, so for us we are still fighting the "medical wars" with our Asian nemesis.

That said, we have no regrets. We were proud to answer the call and play a vital role in Operation Warp Speed. One in every two doses of the COVID vaccine was administered using our needles. By some estimates, the vaccination program—the fastest in the history of the world—prevented three million deaths and incalculable incidents of illness and other debilitating conditions caused by the disease.[108]

So there is much to celebrate around the success of OWS. However, if you pardon the cliché, while we all collectively won the battle, the war is just beginning.

What Comes Next

Shortages of medicines, wheelchairs, and other essential items persist. These shortages aren't as dire as during the pandemic, but they are a stark reminder of the weakness of the supply line. We try to plug the gaps when we can, but that has its limits: too many cracks in the dam, and the whole thing bursts.

The silver lining of this chaos is that it can no longer be ignored: the public as well as government officials and politicians are slowly waking up to the fact that our medical supply is at risk. We are like a sick patient hooked up to IV lines and machinery that keep our lungs breathing and heart beating, but Beijing has its hand on the cord, and can yank it out of the wall whenever it likes.

The nation lacks a coherent, adequately forceful strategy to contain China and wean ourselves off our addiction to its manufacturing, but at least China is part of the political discourse. It seems that the foreign policy establishment is shifting away from its complacent posture to a more realist engagement with our ascendant, and increasingly belligerent, East Asian rival. China's long-term project to knock the United States off its perch as the reigning superpower can only occur in the face of our own inaction. We must approach Chinese diplomacy more thoughtfully, starting with a strategic rethinking of supply chain—and not just masks and gloves, but raw materials, critical drugs, and microchips.

Meanwhile, a shifting geopolitical terrain introduces fresh challenges to both foreign affairs and world trade. The Russia-Ukraine war has forged new diplomatic fault lines, tested long-standing alliances, and inadvertently bolstered others (such as America's relationship with its European allies). That conflict has sent economic shockwaves throughout the global economy, reminding us once again how vulnerable and easily disrupted our vital supply chains are. The world is small: bombs in Dnipro and Kiev translate to grain shortages in Egypt, or a backlog of wheelchair orders in the U.S.

The war in Ukraine, along with the pandemic and other recent events, have lent credence to the notion that we are about to enter, or have entered, an era of deglobalization—a reversal of forty years of transnational integration, free trade, and the (relatively) free movement of people and capital over once-impervious nation-state borders.

The United States was not the only country for whom COVID was a wake-up call regarding its reliance on offshore manufacturing, and not just for medical supplies but virtually every industry. Might it be wise, pundits ask, to return to an era where we make (most of) what we need? Doesn't a system with so many transnational, interlocking dependencies put us all at risk?

The supply chain question, combined with the continual lament blaming deindustrialization for the loss of jobs and a shrinking middle class, have made "reshoring" a rallying cry across the ideological and socioeconomic spectra.

So is the globalized system we have all grown accustomed to falling apart? And if so, what will a "deglobalized" world really look like? Globalization is not some kind of inevitable "end of history" (in the spirit of Francis Fukuyama) stage of human development. It may feel like that, especially for my children's generation, which has never known anything else. But globalization is not necessarily a permanent fixture; it is simply one way of organizing society and commerce that can theoretically be dismantled, or simply erode in response to historical circumstances, over time. As Smil writes in *How the World Really Works:*[109]

"Perhaps the greatest misconception about globalization is that it is a historical inevitability preordained by economic and social evolution. Not so—globalization is not, as former U.S. President [Bill Clinton] claimed, 'the economic equivalent of a force of nature, like wind or water'; it is just another human construct, and there is now a growing consensus that, in some ways, it has already gone too far and needs to be readjusted."

Closer to home, private industry is nursing a COVID hangover. Some industries are still recovering. Others will be forever changed. And many once-vibrant companies, especially small and medium-sized businesses, were casualties of the pandemic that are never coming back. Inflation (driven by multiple causes, leading among them a stressed and redefining supply chain) is taking a bite out of everyone's finances. Talk of recession dominates the financial press. The U.S. may be able to avoid a recession in the next year or two, but another one will come eventually. When it does, what does that mean for the project of reshoring? No one is going to pay more money to Buy American in the middle of a recession. It only works if federal action—and money—tips the economic scales so Americans don't have to pay more for what they're accustomed to getting for less.

And in terms of global public health, we are not faring as well as we were before the word "coronavirus" was on everyone's lips. Besides long-term effects in people who've recovered from COVID, there are also secondary effects from overwhelmed healthcare systems (a lack of general preventative screenings, undiagnosed illnesses, reduced treatment of other conditions), as well as lockdowns and the related physical and mental health implications.

The pandemic was a wide-scale tragedy. We could quote figures about the virus's casualties, but citing the statistics—of people sickened or permanently debilitated, people young and old, strong and weak, whose bodies succumbed as the virus ravaged their lungs (or kidneys, or brain, or other organs)—does not really convey the pandemic's reach. Numbers that big simply become abstract. It's easier to understand the virus by thinking of your friend or neighbor or colleague, or maybe you, who had it. While you survived, you probably felt some fear—if not for yourselves, then for your loved ones. Most of us fared okay. But we were all affected in some way.

It's said that crisis brings out the best and the worst in people, and I experienced this myself in 2020-2021. We fought daily battles with shady, selfish, and sometimes downright amoral people, but we also met decent people all over the world.

There were people like Ryan Croley, a consummate professional, and Brian Durant, who postponed retirement just to help with a vital mission. Or Lisa Noonemire, the hospital administrator in Kansas, who made call after call after call to protect the elderly patients under her care. During COVID, there must have been many unsung Durants and Croleys and Noonemires in every country—ordinary people trying to do what's best for their community.

Even the China factory chairman, though he works at the behest of the CCP, was simply trying to run an honest business and serve his clients and, to a broader extent, his community.

They weren't heroes or even notably altruistic; just decent folks fulfilling their duty without trying to interfere with others doing the same.

My work with OWS made me realize that we are part of a global community. Within that community, there is competition: economic, ideological, etc. People will, naturally, take care of those close to them first. That means their families, followed by their local communities, followed by their nation; concentric circles of widening self-interest. Everyone has their own interests, and we have to recognize that fact.

But there is room for everyone, I think. Our interests are not necessarily disharmonious, even in a world of limited resources. Limited doesn't have to mean *scarce.* We should build a world where the worthwhile aim of feeding your family and helping your community get by, whether in the extreme conditions of a pandemic or simply day to day, doesn't put you at cross-purposes with your counterparts in other countries who are doing the same. We should build a world where news of a health emergency is not the starting pistol shot that kicks off an every-country-for-themselves race to the bottom in which the crookedest and most rapacious operatives hold all the leverage.

If any good can come out of COVID, it is that it has jolted us into action, forced us to face a complicated set of problems we had let fester: Our lack of health preparedness. Our incomplete and inconsistent healthcare system that serves some people very well but leaves others out in the cold. Our dependence on China, India, and other states, and the helplessness that cripples even the world's sole superpower when ships stop shipping, planes stop flying, miners stop mining, and factories go dark.

EPILOGUE

iRemedy continues to do its part to serve this mission. We're committed to enhancing our AI based supply chain platform so that we can build the largest, smartest healthcare products catalog in the world. We believe the solution to the medical supply chain starts with knowledge and our intent is to know everything about every product—from details on raw materials, to manufacturing and distribution. With this intelligence we can work with government and industry partners to find ways to add resilience to the medical supply chain. Additionally, iRemedy's marketplace provides go-to-market services for new, domestic based manufacturers that are entering the market.

American entrepreneurs are beginning to make moves, despite the hindrances of post-COVID economics. Large healthcare providers, biotech firms, and government partners in Health and Human Services and Defense are all beginning to cautiously explore and embrace the possibilities. I know about ten companies that have opened, or are in the process of opening, small factories. Mostly they're producing items such as isolation gowns, gloves, saline bags, N95 respirators, crutches, and wheelchairs, rather than drugs, and most of them still depend on foreign-sourced components, but it's an encouraging sign. Five years ago, no one in the industry was talking about this, much less doing it. Now, we may be on the cusp of a "reboot" of healthcare manufacturing. It won't happen on its own, without the kind of federal support, political muscle, and private-public coalition building we previously talked about. But it can be done.

We just need a shot in the arm.

ACKNOWLEDGEMENTS

In penning "The Last of Us," our team had to first navigate the challenging reality of distributing over a billion medical supplies manufactured in China amidst the most severe health crisis of the twenty-first century. This book is the synthesis of insights gleaned from that Herculean task, combined with two decades of expertise in the medical supply chain, to explore the ramifications for our national security.

Foremost, I must express my profound gratitude to my son, Anthony Paquin. In his capacity as Vice President of Sales at our medical supply company, he was instrumental in securing the Operation Warp Speed (OWS) government contract. His unwavering dedication saw him play a key role in managing the delivery of over one billion needles and syringes, as he worked with the team round-the-clock for more than a year. Furthermore, his relentless support as a researcher, editor, and collaborator was pivotal in bringing this manuscript to fruition. His vigor and acumen were the bedrock upon which both OWS and this volume rest; this book would not have happened without him.

My brother, Gary Paquin, co-founder of iRemedy, provided indispensable support throughout this intricate journey. My wife, Keisha, was an unwavering pillar amidst the relentless barrage of calls, crises, and deadlines that accompanied our mission. Amanda Somsy, iRemedy's Chief Financial Officer, together with her dedicated team, endured an extraordinary measure of stress and upheaval to ensure our modest enterprise met its objectives. Her commitment was crucial to our success.

Our narrative owes its clarity and engagement to the editorial acumen of Stephen Power and Amanda Barnett, whose guidance was instrumental in sculpting our account. David Ferris, in particular, deserves special mention; his prowess in comprehending, articulating, and refining our account surpassed all expectations.

Adversity has a unique way of introducing us to the finest people. Ryan Croley, a retired Navy SEAL, and Jeantelle Duhon, a Navy veteran, exemplify such sterling character. Ryan and Jeantelle were critically important to managing the complex OWS contracts. It is because of individuals like them—genuine, resolute, and dedicated problem-solvers, deeply invested in the welfare of their fellow Americans—that my faith in the future of our nation is unwavering.

NOTES

1 Michelle L. Holshue, Chas DeBolt, Scott Lindquist, et al., "First Case of 2019 Novel Coronavirus in the United States," *New England Journal of Medicine* 2020; 382:929-936, DOI: 10.1056/NEJMoa2001191,
https://www.nejm.org/doi/full/10.1056/NEJMoa2001191

2 While this individual was the first *confirmed* case of COVID inside the United States at the time, later studies found that the virus was already present on the west coast as early as December 2019. See Sridhar V Basavaraju, Monica E Patton, and Kacie Grimm, et al., "Serologic Testing of US Blood Donations to Identify Severe Acute Respiratory Syndrome Coronavirus 2 (SARS-CoV-2)–Reactive Antibodies: December 2019–January 2020," *Clinical Infectious Diseases, Volume 72*, Issue 12, 15 June 2021,
https://academic.oup.com/cid/article/72/12/e1004/6012472?login=false

3 https://www.pharmaceutical-technology.com/news/us-pharmacopeia-report-high-reliance-indian-manufacturers-api/

4 https://asia.nikkei.com/static/vdata/infographics/chinavaccine-3/

5 https://asia.nikkei.com/static/vdata/infographics/chinavaccine-3/

6 https://www.wsj.com/articles/how-the-u-s-ceded-control-of-drug-supplies-to-china-11596634936

7 https://www.politico.com/news/2019/12/20/policymakers-worry-china-drug-exports-088126

8 https://www.bloomberg.com/news/articles/2022-03-29/generic-drug-supply-in-u-s-is-very-reliant-on-india#xj4y7vzkg

9 https://qualitymatters.usp.org/geographic-concentration-pharmaceutical-manufacturing

10 https://asia.nikkei.com/static/vdata/infographics/chinavaccine-3/

11 Rosemary Gibson & Janardan Prasad Singh, *China Rx: Exposing the Risks of America's Dependence on China for Medicine,* Buffalo: Prometheus Books, 2022.

12 https://www.bloomberg.com/news/articles/2022-03-29/generic-drug-supply-in-u-s-is-very-reliant-on-india#xj4y7vzkg

13 Adam E. M. Eltorai, Henry Fox, Emily McGurrin, and Stephanie Guang, "Microchips in Medicine: Current and Future Applications," *Biomed Res Int.* 2016; 2016: 1743472, 2016 Jun 7. doi: 10.1155/2016/1743472

14 https://www.forbes.com/sites/katharinabuchholz/2022/07/27/greater-china-dominates-global-microchip-exports-infographic/?sh=580e194f3e3d

15 https://www.foxbusiness.com/healthcare/chip-shortage-very-real-critical-challenge-healthcare-hologic-ceo

16 https://www.wsj.com/articles/pacemaker-ultrasound-companies-seek-priority-amid-chip-shortage-11633258802

17 https://www.wsj.com/articles/pacemaker-ultrasound-companies-seek-priority-amid-chip-shortage-11633258802

18 https://www.mddionline.com/materials/rare-earth-metal-shortage-could-spell-trouble-medtech-firms

19 https://www.dw.com/en/how-chinas-mines-rule-the-market-of-critical-raw-materials/a-57148375

20 https://www.dw.com/en/how-chinas-mines-rule-the-market-of-critical-raw-materials/a-57148375

21 https://www.dw.com/en/how-chinas-mines-rule-the-market-of-critical-raw-materials/a-57148375

22https://khn.org/news/article/loan-closets-medical-equipment-shortage-supply-chain-problem/

23 Augusta Saraiva, "Biggest US Ports Rank as World's Least Efficient for Containers," Bloomberg, May 25, 2022, https://www.bloomberg.com/news/articles/2022-05-25/biggest-us-ports-rank-as-world-s-least-efficient-for-containers#xj4y7vzkg

24 Matt Field, "The Strategic National Stockpile failed during COVID and monkeypox. Will it come through next time?," Bulletin of the Atomic Scientists, Sept. 29, 2022, https://thebulletin.org/2022/09/the-strategic-national-stockpile-failed-during-COVID-and-monkeypox-will-it-come-through-next-time

25 Vaclav Smil, *How the World Really Works: The Science Behind How We Got Here and Where We're Going*, New York: Viking Press, 2022, p. 133.

26 Daniella Genovese, "Inflation, supply chain shortages making it harder, more expensive to obtain needed medical equipment," FOX Business, April 25, 2022, https://www.foxbusiness.com/lifestyle/cme-medica-equipment-costs

27 "Coronavirus in the U.S.: Latest Map and Case Count," New York Times, https://www.nytimes.com/interactive/2021/us/COVID-cases.html

28 Leonardo M. Millefiori et al., "COVID-19 impact on global maritime mobility," *Scientific Reports*, 11, 18039 (2021),, https://www.nature.com/articles/s41598-021-97461-7

29 Ben van der Merwe, "Weekly data: How COVID-19 disrupted global shipping," Investment Monitor, Sept. 13, 2021,https://www.investmentmonitor.ai/analysis/COVID-global-shipping-container-shortage

30 Vaclav Smil, *How the World Really Works: The Science Behind How We Got Here and Where We're Going*, New York: Viking Press, 2022, p. 105

31 Yi Wen, "China's Rapid Rise: From Backward Agrarian Society to Industrial Powerhouse in Just 35 Years," Federal Reserve Bank of St. Louis, April 11, 2016, https://www.stlouisfed.org/publications/regional-economist/april-2016/chinas-rapid-rise-from-backward-agrarian-society-to-industrial-powerhouse-in-just-35-years

32 Michael Brown and Pavneet Singh, "China's Technology Transfer Strategy: How Chinese Investments in Emerging Technology Enable A Strategic Competitor to Access the Crown Jewels of U.S. Innovation," Defense Innovation Unit Experimental, January 2018, p. 3.

33 Sutter et al., *COVID-19: China Medical Supply Chains and Broader Trade Issues,* Congressional Research Service, Dec. 20, 2020, p. 1

[34] Anshu Siripurapu, "What is the Defense PRoduction Act," Council on Foreign Relations, Dec. 22, 2021, https://www.cfr.org/in-brief/what-defense-production-act

[35] Bureau of International Labor Affairs, "Against Their Will: The Situation in Xinjiang," U.S. Department of Labor, https://www.dol.gov/agencies/ilab/against-their-will-the-situation-in-xinjiang, n.d.

[36] Ibid.

[37] Michael Pillsbury, *The Hundred-Year Marathon: China's Secret Strategy to Replace America as the Global Superpower*, St. Martin's Griffin, 2016.

[38] Ibid., p. 44.

[39] Ibid., p. 47.

[40] Clay Chandler and Grady McGregor, "When will China overtake the U.S. as the world's largest economy? Maybe never," Fortune, Sept. 28, 2021, https://fortune.com/2021/09/28/china-economy-gdp-overtake-us-when-never/

[41] Ibid.

[42] *The Economist*, "Is China already the world's most dominant economy?," Sept. 18, 2021, https://www.economist.com/finance-and-economics/2021/09/18/is-china-already-the-worlds-most-dominant-economy

[43] Tom Hancock, "China's economy slowly edges toward world dominance," Bloomberg, March 2, 2021, https://www.bloomberg.com/news/storythreads/2021-03-03/china-s-economy-slowly-edges-toward-world-dominance

[44] Macrotrends, "China GDP growth rate, 1961-2021, retrieved on Nov. 9, 2021, https://www.macrotrends.net/countries/CHN/china/gdp-growth-rate

[45] Ibid.

[46] European Commission Competence Centre on Foresight, "China's R&D Strategy," n.d., https://knowledge4policy.ec.europa.eu/foresight/topic/expanding-influence-east-south/industry-science-innovation_en

[47] Michael E. O'Hanlon, "What the Pentagon's new report on China means for US strategy — including on Taiwan," Brookings Institution, Sept. 4., 2020, https://www.brookings.edu/blog/order-from-chaos/2020/09/04/what-the-pentagons-new-report-on-china-means-for-u-s-strategy-including-on-taiwan/

[48] European Commission Competence Centre on Foresight, "China's R&D Strategy," n.d., https://knowledge4policy.ec.europa.eu/foresight/topic/expanding-influence-east-south/industry-science-innovation_en

[49] Sutter et al., *COVID-19: China Medical Supply Chains and Broader Trade Issues,* Congressional Research Service, Dec. 20, 2020

[50] Tom Hancock, "These Are the Megaprojects in China's $1 Trillion Infrastructure Plan," Bloomberg, Aug. 25, 2022, https://www.bloomberg.com/news/features/2022-08-25/how-china-will-spend-1-trillion-on-infrastructure-to-boost-economy

[51] James McBride and Anshu Siripurapu, "The State of U.S. Infrastructure," Council on Foreign Relations, Nov. 8, 2021, https://www.cfr.org/backgrounder/state-us-infrastructure

[52] Michael Pillsbury, , p. 47

[53] Michael E. O'Hanlon, "What the Pentagon's new report on China means for US strategy — including on Taiwan," Brookings Institution, Sept. 4, 2020,

https://www.brookings.edu/blog/order-from-chaos/2020/09/04/what-the-pentagons-new-report-on-china-means-for-u-s-strategy-including-on-taiwan/
[54] Business Insider, "Ranked: The world's 20 strongest militaries," July 13, 2021, https://www.businessinsider.in/defense/ranked-the-worlds-20-strongest-militaries/slidelist/51930339.cms
[55] https://www.bbc.com/news/world-asia-china-59600475
[56] Ibid.
[57] Ibid.
[58] Wendell Minnick, "Book Review: The Hundred-Year Marathon," *Defense News*, Jan. 27, 2015, https://www.defensenews.com/opinion/intercepts/2015/01/27/book-review-the-hundred-year-marathon/
[59] Michael Pillsbury, *The Hundred-Year Marathon: China's Secret Strategy to Replace America as the Global Superpower*, St. Martin's Griffin, 2016.
[60] Patricia Kim, "China's Search for Allies," Foreign Affairs, Nov. 15, 2021, https://www.foreignaffairs.com/articles/china/2021-11-15/chinas-search-allies
[61] *The Economist*, "China unveils its vision of a global security order," May 5, 2022, https://www.economist.com/china/2022/05/05/china-unveils-its-vision-of-a-global-security-order&cd=2&hl=en&ct=clnk&gl=hu&client=firefox-b-d
[62] Ibid.
[63] Eleanor Albert, "China's Big Bet on Soft Power," Council on Foreign Relations, Feb. 9, 2018, https://www.cfr.org/backgrounder/chinas-big-bet-soft-power
[64] Blake Simmons, Kevin P. Gallagher, and Rebecca Ray, "China is financing infrastructure projects around the world – many could harm nature and Indigenous communities", The Conversation, Sept. 22, 2021, https://theconversation.com/china-is-financing-infrastructure-projects-around-the-world-many-could-harm-nature-and-indigenous-communities-168060
[65] Plamen Tonchev, "2 Major Traps on China's Path to Global Leadership," *The Diplomat*, Sept. 1, 2022, https://thediplomat.com/2022/09/2-major-traps-on-chinas-path-to-global-leadership/
[66] Ibid.
[67] https://foreignpolicy.com/2022/11/01/zero-covid-china-economic-problems-demographics/
[68] Ibid.
[69] https://www.reuters.com/world/china/chinas-population-shrinks-first-time-since-1961-2023-01-17/
[70] Pillsbury, p. 216
[71] Anna Edney, "U.S. Drug Supply Is Even More Reliant on India Than Thought," Bloomberg, March 29, 2022, https://www.bloomberg.com/news/articles/2022-03-29/generic-drug-supply-in-u-s-is-very-reliant-on-india
[72] Ibid.
[73] https://www.bloomberg.com/news/features/2022-04-11/india-hopes-pharma-city-will-break-china-s-grip-on-drug-industry#xj4y7vzkg
[74] https://www.cnbc.com/2022/05/27/india-needs-to-fill-china-gaps-to-become-the-pharmacy-of-the-world.html

75 https://www.bloomberg.com/news/features/2022-04-11/india-hopes-pharma-city-will-break-china-s-grip-on-drug-industry#xj4y7vzkg

76 Gibson and Singh, *China RX,* p. 36.

77 "Top 10 Pharma Companies in India by Market Capitalization," GlobalData.com, https://www.globaldata.com/companies/top-companies-by-sector/healthcare/india-companies-by-market-cap/

78 For comparison's sake, if a foreign drug firm wants to do business in the U.S., they typically have to set up a U.S.-based entity to represent them in obtaining the various required registrations. Many Chinese and Indian manufacturers operate what are essentially "shell" corporations that are listed on their FDA registration etc. There is an entire industry in the U.S. where Chinese representatives become "U.S. agents" for Chinese companies in need of U.S. representation.

79 https://www.wolterskluwer.com/en/expert-insights/doing-business-in-india

80 https://www.dw.com/en/indias-massive-pharma-industry-hounded-by-scandals/a-63561810

81 https://www.dw.com/en/indias-massive-pharma-industry-hounded-by-scandals/a-63561810

82 Ibid.

83 https://www.politico.eu/article/indias-stance-on-the-ukraine-war-makes-little-sense/

84 https://news.gallup.com/poll/1627/china.aspx

85 https://www.cnbc.com/2020/11/09/president-elect-biden-coronavirus-advisor-osterholm-says-us-is-about-to-enter-covid-hell.html

86 Karen Goldschmidt & Kelsey Stasko, "The downstream effects of the COVID-19 pandemic: The supply chain failure, a wicked problem," *J Pediatr Nurs.* 2022 July-August; 65: 29–32. Published online 2022 Apr 18. doi: 10.1016/j.pedn.2022.04.001, https://www.ncbi.nlm.nih.gov/pmc/articles/PMC9014739/

87 https://samscoalition.org/

88 Dylan Scott, "Why does the US keep running out of medicine?", *Vox*, Dec. 5, 2022, www.vox.com/platform/amp/policy-and-politics/23484040/rsv-flu-amoxicillin-tamiflu-abuterol-drug-shortages

89 Wallace J. Hopp, Lisa Brown, & Carolyn Shore (Eds.), National Academies of Sciences, Engineering, and Medicine. 2022. Building Resilience into the Nation's Medical Product Supply Chains. Washington, DC: The National Academies Press. https://doi.org/10.17226/26420, p. 97

90 Wallace J. Hopp, Lisa Brown, Ibid.

91 Larry Rosania, "Heparin crisis 2008: a tipping point for increased FDA enforcement in the pharma sector?," Food and Drug Law Journal, 2010;65(3):489-501, ii., https://pubmed.ncbi.nlm.nih.gov/24479237/

92 Rosemay Gibson & Janardan Prasad Singh, *ChinaRX*

93 Ibid.

94 Wallace J. Hopp, Lisa Brown, & Carolyn Shore (Eds.), National Academies of Sciences, Engineering, and Medicine. 2022. Building Resilience into the Nation's Medical Product Supply Chains. Washington, DC: The National Academies Press. https://doi.org/10.17226/26420

---

[95] Ibid, p. 97

[96] Gibson & Singh, p. 60.

[97] Ibid.

[98] "Fact Sheet: FDA at a Glance," Food and Drug Administration, November 2021, https://www.fda.gov/about-fda/fda-basics/fact-sheet-fda-glance

[99] Michael O'Hanlon, "Can China Take Taiwan?", Brookings Institution, August 2022,

[100] https://asia.nikkei.com/Spotlight/Caixin/China-creates-massive-state-owned-logistics-group

[101] Gibson and Singh, *China Rx,* p. 38

[102] https://www.warren.senate.gov/oversight/letters/warren-lawmakers-call-on-commerce-dept-to-prevent-chips-funds-from-being-used-to-subsidize-corporate-stock-buybacks

[103] Sardella, Anthony, "U.S. GENERIC PHARMACEUTICAL MANUFACTURERAVAILABLE CAPACITY RESEARCH SURVEY," Center for Analytics and Business Insights, Washington University in St. Louis, Sept. 30, , https://wustl.app.box.com/s/32e1w52bgajp6pz22gf4vjotj78997uk

[104] "Pharmaceutical Manufacturing in America," U.S. Dept. of Health and Human Services, https://www.medicalcountermeasures.gov/barda/influenza-and-emerging-infectious-diseases/coronavirus/pharmaceutical-manufacturing-in-america/?filter=infrastructureExpansion

[105] https://www.cnbc.com/2020/09/29/5-charts-show-how-the-us-and-chinese-economies-depend-on-each-other.html

[106] Gibson & Singh, *China Rx*

[107] "Letter to Majority Leader Schumer, Speaker Pelosi, Leader McConnell, and Leader McCarthy," Nov. 15, 2022, https://www.ada.org/-/media/project/ada-organization/ada/ada-org/files/advocacy/221115_multiorgpreventpandemics_signonletter.pdf?rev=fd8e2437 75cd4456870f5be56b9b9a82&hash=843655B428F240F2515492CCAB46A30C

[108] https://www.statnews.com/2022/12/13/covid-vaccines-prevented-3-million-deaths/

[109] Smil, *How the World Really Works,* p. 105.

INDEX

INDEX

ABOUT THE AUTHOR

A serial entrepreneur, industry pioneer, sought-after speaker and international healthcare consultant, Tony Paquin has founded and led numerous public and private companies and organizations. Tony is the author of *The Retail Healthcare Revolution*, published in 2009.

Paquin is also a leading software and technology designer, patented inventor and architect of numerous healthcare and insurance technology solutions. Currently, he serves as President and Chief Executive Officer of iRemedy Healthcare, a technology firm that has built an artificial intelligence based medical supplies marketplace.

Previously, he served as President and CEO of Medinex, Inc., a healthcare technology company he co-founded and took public on the NASDAQ, and prior to its sale to CNA Financial Corporation, he was the co-founder, President and CEO of Agency One, an insurance technology company.

Tony has participated in panel discussions at the Naval War College and has advised and consulted with the senior leaders of hundreds of healthcare and insurance companies. He has worked with governors, senators, and other public officials and their staffs, and has been a candidate for the U.S. House of Representatives.